Write first 3

Progression in cross-curricular writing skills

Ray Barker
Christine Moorcroft

First published in 2001 by:

Nelson Thornes
Delta Place
27 Bath Road
CHELTENHAM GL53 7TH
United Kingdom

01 02 03 04 05 / 10 9 8 7 6 5 4 3 2 1

A catalogue record for this book is available from the British Library.

ISBN 0 7487 6154 3

Developed and produced by Start to Finish
Typeset by Paul Manning
Printed and bound in Italy by Canale

Acknowledgements

TEXTS Unit 1: from Terry Pratchett, *The Unadulterated Cat* (Victor Gollancz, 1989), reprinted by permission of The Orion Publishing Group; **Unit 2:** from George Orwell, *Homage to Catalonia* (Secker & Warburg, 1937), © George Orwell, 1973, reprinted by permission of Bill Hamilton as the Literary Executor of the Estate of the Late Sonia Brownell Orwell and Secker & Warburg Ltd; **Unit 4:** from Louis de Bernières, *Caption Corelli's Mandolin* (Secker & Warburg, 1994), reprinted by permission of The Random House Group Ltd; **Unit 5:** from Stephen Fay and Eric Jacobs, *Smithfield: A Market of Our Time* (Corporation of London, 1997), reprinted by permission of the publisher; **Unit 6:** 'Alcoholic Drinks', rules from the British Codes of Advertising and Sales Promotion, from the website of the Advertising Standards Authority, reprinted by permission of the ASA; **Unit 7:** from Oliver Sacks, *The Man Who Mistook His Wife For a Hat* (Picador, 1985), reprinted by permission of The Wylie Agency, London; **Unit 8:** from Sue Townsend, *The Secret Diary of Adrian Mole Aged 13⅓*(Methuen, 1982), © Sue Townsend 1982, 1984, reprinted by permission of Curtis Brown Ltd; **Unit 9:** from *A Miner's Diary of 1907*, edited by Alastair Robertson (Hundy Publications, 2000), reprinted by permission of Alastair Robertson; **Unit 10:** from Franz Kafka, *Metamorphosis*, translated by Edwin Muir (Secker & Warburg, 1949), reprinted by permission of The Random House Group Ltd; **Unit 12:** from H.G. Wells, *War of the Worlds* (Heinemann, 1898), reprinted by permission of A.P. Watt Ltd on behalf of the Literary Executors of the Estate of H.G. Wells; **Unit 13:** from Steven Saylor, *Roman Blood* (Robinson Publishing, 1997), reprinted by permission of Constable & Robinson Ltd; **Unit 14:** from Jack Shaefer, 'Shane' from *Shane and Other Stories* (Penguin, 1989), reprinted by permission of the publisher; **Unit 15:** from William Golding, *Hot Gates* (Faber & Faber, 1984), reprinted by permission of the publisher; **Unit 16:** from Richard Feynman, *Surely You're Joking, Mr Feynman!: Adventures of a Curious Character* (Vintage, 1992), reprinted by permission of Random House Group Ltd; **Unit 17:** from Bill Bryson, *Notes From A Small Island* (Black Swan, 1995), reprinted by permission of Transworld Publishers; **Unit 18:** from Ian Jenkins, *Greek and Roman Life* (British Museum Publications, 1986), © The Trustees of the British Museum, reprinted by permission of British Museum Press, London; **Unit 20:** Ray Bradbury, 'Embroidery' from *The Golden Apples of the Sun* (Heinemann Educational Books, 1990), © 1951 by Stadium Publishing, renewed 1979 by Ray Bradbury, reprinted by permission of Don Congdon Associates Inc.; **Unit 21:** from *The Letters of Vincent Van Gogh*, edited by Mark Roskill (Fontana, 1967), reprinted by permission of HarperCollins Publishers; **Unit 23:** from Susan Irvine, *Perfume: The Creation and Allure of Classic Fragrances* (Aurum Press, 1995), reprinted by permission of Haldane Mason on behalf of the author; **Unit 24:** 'Holocaust Day: a piece of Labour hypocrisy?' from *The Week* (3 February 2001), reprinted by permission of the publisher; **Unit 25:** from Department of Health 'Keep Warm Keep Well' leaflet (Department of Health, 2000), reprinted by permission of Department of Health Publications Information Unit, London; **Unit 27:** Daniel Hannan, 'The problem pill' from *The Daily Telegraph* (2 January 2001), reprinted by permission of Telegraph Group Ltd; **Unit 28:** from film review of *The Claim* by Damien Love in *The Scotsman* (8 February 2001), reprinted by permission of the author; **Unit 30:** from Ann Widdecombe, speech to the 1999 Conservative Party conference, reprinted by permission of the author.

PHOTOGRAPHS Page 18: courtesy of James Morris and the Corporation of London; **pages 29 and 30:** courtesy of Alastair Robertson; **page 35:** courtesy of AKG London; **page 70:** courtesy of The Art Archive/National Gallery, London/Eileen Tweedy; **page 78:** courtesy of AKG London; **page 89:** courtesy of Aquarius; **page 94:** courtesy of the Conservative Party Press Office.

Every effort has been made to trace or contact all copyright holders. The publishers would be pleased to rectify any omissions brought to their notice at the earliest opportunity.

Illustrations by: **Tim Archbold** (pages 4–5, 25–6); **Charlotte Combe** (pages 13–15, 22, 32–3, 65–7); **Tom Cross** (pages 54–5, 62, 75); **Linda Jeffrey** (pages 28, 52, 69, 71, 73, 76, 86, 88–9, 91–2); **Carol Jonas** (pages 10, 38–9, 44–6, 55, 63, 83–4); **Ruth Palmer** (pages 7–8, 41–2, 48–50, 57–60).

Contents

1 Audience and purpose: comedy

How to get a cat

1. Adverts in the Post Office

Five adorable tabby kittens
Just ready to leave Mum
Free to Good Home

Yes. Please, *Please* Phone, because they're all big and fighting with one another and some of the males are beginning to take a sophisticated interest in Mum. Do not be fooled into believing that you will need to turn up bearing evidence of regular church-going and sober habits; good home in this case means anyone who doesn't actually arrive in a van marked

J Torquemada and Sons, Furriers.

If you answer the ad you'll find there's one kitten left.

There's always one kitten left. You spend ages trying to figure out what it was that made the previous four purchasers leave it behind. Eventually you will find out. Nevertheless, Adverts in the Post Office are a good way of acquiring your basic cat.

2. Adverts in posh cat magazines

Pretty much like (1.) except that the word 'adorable' probably won't be used and the word 'free' *certainly* won't be used. Not to be contemplated by anyone on a normal income.

The cats acquired in this way are often very decorative, but if that's all you want a cat for then a trip to the nearest urban motorway with a paint scraper will do the business. Pedigree cats talk a lot – catownerspeak for yowling softly – and tend

Glossary

Torquemada Tomás de Torquemada (1420–98), First Inquisitor-General of Spain, who showed great cruelty and was responsible for an estimated 2,000 burnings

to rip curtains. Being so highly bred, some of them are mentally unstable. A friend had a cat which thought it was a saucepan. But, because it was very expensive and more highly bred than Queen Victoria, it thought it was a saucepan with *style*.

3. Buying a house in the Country

A very reliable way of acquiring a cat. It'll normally turn up within the first year, with a smug expression that suggests it is a little surprised to see you here. It doesn't belong to the previous occupants, none of the neighbours recognise it, but it seems perfectly at home.

4. The Cats' Home

Another very popular source, especially just after Christmas and the summer holiday period, when their sales are on. Despite the fact that you can barely hear her on the phone for the background of yowling, the harassed young lady will probably take rather more pains than the average Post Office Advert cat seller to ensure you haven't actually got skinning knives in your pocket. Often no payment, just a voluntary donation – made at pistol point. You will be offered a variety of furry kittens, but the cat for you is the one-year-old spayed female lurking at the back of the cage with a worried expression who will show her appreciation by piddling in the car all the way home.

5. Inheritance

These cats come with a selection of bowls, half a tin of the most expensive cat food on the market, a basket and a small woolly thing with a bell in it. They will then spend two weeks under the bed in the spare room. Try to get it out and it could be *you* in the hospital having skin from your buttocks grafted onto your arm. Cats are not always inherited from dead people. If the previous owner is still alive, the Real cat will probably be accompanied by a list of its likes and dislikes. Throw it away. They're just fads anyway. Try to avoid inheriting cats unless they come with a five-figure legacy, or at least the expectation of one.

6. Joint ownership

Do you know where your cat spends its time when it's not at home? It's worth checking with more distant neighbours that they don't have a cat with the same size and colouring. It can happen. We once knew two households who for years both thought they owned the same cat, which spent its time commuting between food bowls.

An interesting fact about acquiring cats is that the things are, by and large, either virtually free or very expensive. It's as if the motor industry had nothing between the moped and the Porsche.

from *The Unadulterated Cat*
by Terry Pratchett

Read on!

1 Tell the group a joke. Note how your audience reacts. What does this tell you about the difficulty of writing comedy for an audience?

2 Does your audience depend upon anything other than the quality of the joke itself? If so, what?

3 Do fashions in humour change? What did you find amusing as a child which you do not find funny now?

4 Consider any 'comic' scenes in a Shakespeare play you know. What prevents you from finding them amusing? Which features in these scenes remain amusing four hundred years later?

5 When you see a comic character being punched or falling over, you often laugh. Is this cruel?

6 Find something amusing in each section of the passage and explain why it is amusing. Sort your responses on a chart:

Comedy of character	Comedy of situation	Comedy of language

7 Try the same activity again, listing comic things in a film you have seen recently. Are the kinds of comedy different in each genre? What does this tell you about the way different genres need to match their different audiences?

Write on!

One reason why the passage is amusing is that we have all had some experience of dealing with animals and can see the 'truth' behind the jokes. The other reason is that the writer uses language very carefully.

1 Look up these words in a dictionary: tone, satire, irony, joke, absurd, juxtaposition.

2 Find examples of these in the passage, if possible. Explain how they create the humour. Are any of these comic features *not* represented in this passage?

3 Write a similar but shorter passage, using a similar format: 'Two ways to get a dog'.

   • Use the same plan, kinds of detail and tone.
   • Read the passage to the group. Do they find it amusing? If not, why not?

Over to you!

Using the tone and language of the passage as a model, write a comic piece about what happens when people bring their cat home.

   • How does the cat become the 'boss' in the house?
   • How do the humans react?
   • What situations occur?
   • Consider the various types of comedy and how you can create situations to exploit these. Use the Activity Sheet to help.

2 Describing personal experiences

George Orwell describes what it was like to be shot during the Spanish Civil War of the 1930s.

The whole experience of being hit by a bullet is very interesting and I think worth describing in detail.

It was at the corner of the parapet, at five o'clock in the morning. This was always a dangerous time, because we had the dawn at our backs, and if you stuck your head above the parapet it was clearly outlined against the sky. I was talking to the sentries preparatory to changing the guard. Suddenly, in the very middle of saying something, I felt – it is very hard to describe what I felt, though I remember it with the utmost vividness.

Roughly speaking it was the sensation of being *at the centre of* an explosion. There seemed to be a loud bang and a blinding flash of light all round me, and I felt a tremendous shock – no pain, only a violent shock, such as you get from an electric terminal; with it a sense of utter weakness, a feeling of being stricken and shrivelled up to nothing. The sandbags in front of me receded into immense distance. I fancy you would feel much the same if you were struck by lightning. I knew immediately that I was hit, but because of the seeming bang and flash I thought it was a rifle nearby that had

gone off accidentally and shot me. All this happened in a space of time much less than a second. The next moment my knees crumpled up and I was falling, my head hitting the ground with a violent bang which, to my relief, did not hurt. I had a numb, dazed feeling, a consciousness of being very badly hurt, but no pain in the ordinary sense.

The American sentry I had been talking to had started forward. "Gosh! Are you hit?" People gathered round. There was the usual fuss. "Lift him up! Where's he hit? Get his shirt open!" etc. etc. The American called for a knife to cut my shirt open. I knew that there was one in my pocket and tried to get it out, but discovered that my right arm was paralysed. Not being in pain, I felt a vague satisfaction. This ought to please my wife, I thought; she had always wanted me to be wounded, which would save me from being killed when the great battle came. It was only now that it occurred to me to wonder where I was hit, and how badly; I could feel nothing, but I was conscious that the bullet had struck me somewhere in the front of the body. When I tried to speak I found that I had no voice, only a faint squeak, but at the second attempt I managed to ask where I

Describing personal experiences

was hit. In the throat, they said. Harry Webb, our stretcher-bearer, had brought a bandage and one of the little bottles of alcohol they gave us for field-dressings. As they lifted me up a lot of blood poured out of my mouth, and I heard a Spaniard behind me say that the bullet had gone clean through my neck. I felt the alcohol, which at ordinary times would sting like the devil, splash on to the wound as a pleasant coolness.

They laid me down again while somebody fetched a stretcher. As soon as I knew that the bullet had gone clean through my neck I took it for granted that I was done for. I had never heard of a man or an animal getting a bullet through the middle of the neck and surviving it. The blood was dribbling out of the corner of my mouth. "The artery's gone," I thought. I wondered how long you last when your carotid artery is cut; not many minutes, presumably. Everything was very blurry. There must have been about two minutes during which I assumed that I was

killed. And that too was interesting – I mean it is interesting to know what your thoughts would be at such a time. My first thought, conventionally enough, was for my wife. My second was a violent resentment at having to leave this world which, when all is said and done, suits me so well. I had time to feel this very vividly. The stupid mischance infuriated me. The meaninglessness of it. To be bumped off, not even in battle, but in this stale corner of the trenches, thanks to a moment's carelessness. I thought, too, of the man who had shot me – wondered what he was like, whether he was a Spaniard or a foreigner, whether he knew he had got me, and so forth. I could not feel any resentment against him. I reflected that as he was a Fascist I would have killed him if I could, but that if he had been taken prisoner and brought before me at this moment I would merely have congratulated him on his good shooting. It may be, though, that if you really were dying your thoughts would be quite different.

They had just got me on to the stretcher when my paralysed right arm came to life and began hurting damnably. At the time I imagined that I must have broken it in falling; but the pain reassured me, for I knew that your sensations do not become acute when you are dying. I began to feel more normal and to be sorry for the four poor devils who were sweating and slithering with the stretcher on their shoulders. It was a mile and a half to the ambulance, and vile going, over lumpy, slippery tracks. I knew what a sweat it was, having helped to carry a wounded man down a day or two earlier. The leaves of the silver poplars which, in places, fringed our trenches, brushed against my face; I thought what a good thing it was to be alive in a world where silver poplars grow. But all the while the pain in my arm was diabolical, making me swear and then try not to swear, because every time I breathed too hard the blood bubbled out of my mouth.

from *Homage to Catalonia*
by George Orwell

Read on!

1 Choose some images from the passage which make vivid to you something you will probably never experience. Discuss their effect.

Image	Effect
Like being at the centre of an explosion	Something you can feel all over – something large and shattering

2 Find examples of how the writer gives you a sense of place and of the era by the detail he uses.

3 Look at the variety of adjectives used in the third paragraph. What do they add to the description of the experience?

4 What sense of the character of the narrator does the passage communicate? Copy and complete the chart.

Feature	What this communicates
What he says	
How he says it	
What he does	
How he reacts	

Write on!

1 In describing something personal, George Orwell makes an appeal to our senses. Find examples of this in the extract and make notes under these headings:

Seeing	Hearing	Feeling

2 To make the experience physical (i.e. you can hear it as well as feel it), the author uses onomatopoeic words. Find examples and explain their effect. For example, 'bubbled' is used to describe blood. This makes the experience almost disgusting. It gives an impression of the injured man breathing through a mouth full of blood.

3 Continue with the description of the experience as he is carried on the stretcher. Use details which appeal to the senses and some onomatopoeic words which make you feel the experience.

Over to you!

Use the structure contained in the passage to write your own description of a personal, painful experience, for example, being in a car crash. The Activity Sheet will help.

• Remember to give the description a sense of place and a sense of time.

• Create a sense of character for your narrator by concentrating on dialogue.

• What do you say? How do you say it? What do others think of you?

3 A sense of place

Wallace Nolasco marries wealthy Mr Poon's daughter, but finds that where he has to live – in the more rural part of the once British-owned Hong Kong ('the colony') – is not all he expects.

The village itself lay in a depression, shaped alarmingly like the mouth of a volcano, which was contoured into the mountain's landward flank. It gave the settlement a deceptive air of impermanence, as if it were liable at any moment to be spewed incandescent into the valley. Despite what topology suggested, the site had been continuously inhabited for over a thousand years. The network of families who inhabited the village – a clan bearing a universal surname – took pride in tracing their lineage through to the common ancestor who had founded the settlement a millennium ago. This was a feat characterised more by ingenuity than scrupulousness. Technically, the bulk of the population were usurpers, although of a standing of more than three centuries. Clues to the original trespass persisted in the extent of the village's fortifications. Most New Territories settlements were surrounded by a wall, or at least its ruins, with perhaps an iron gate and in some cases a moat as well. The village exceeded the conventional quota of defences. It was possible to make out the ruin of two walls, with another more or less standing. There was also a trench, now just a shallow depression, a puddle in the rainy season, which had (according to alternative oral legend) variously contained combustible straw or daubed bamboo spikes. For, once,

pirates had preyed on the coast. To the extent that the Imperial government had declared an evacuation of the coastal area, defined within a perimeter of 50 li from the sea. The original inhabitants had been forcibly removed but, undeterred either by piratical depredations or the proscription of the Canton administration, squatters had moved in. When the owners had returned in depleted numbers a decade later, they had accepted the accomplished fact. Force deployed against the defences reared in their absence would have been pointless.

The village and its defences had never been tested by pirates, which piece of good fortune the villagers had attributed to the beneficent fung shui or spirit of the neighbourhood. Geomancers had identified this as a rampant but avuncular dragon near whose forehead the village was by chance or design situated: the eyes to be found by drawing a straight line through a pair of distant peaks which would bisect the village exactly: the protective coils of the creature winding symmetrically round the mountain, culminating in a potent twist on the plateau. In other words the village was invisible from the sea.

The energy spent in fortifying the village had not been expended in vain, however. Pirates and brigands were an episodic threat; other villages were a constant menace. The invariable state of affairs between neighbouring settlements was rivalry; each had its particular feuds. The village had been engaged in a vendetta, started by an irrigation dispute somewhere around the trime of the Tai Ping rebellion, the details of which were lost in time, against a Hakka settlement seven miles up the valley. The Hakkas, 'guest people', had arrived in the area a few centuries ago. Shortly before the colonial authorities had assumed control of the area, an exceptionally sanguinary battle had been fought in which men of the Hakka village had laid hands on an ornamental cannon, harnessed water buffalo to it, and fired fearsome home-made grape-shot into the village. Souvenirs of this engagement (three shots had embedded themselves intact in the mud walls) were kept in the chief of the village's five ancestral halls. Conveniently breached in places to allow the passage of carts, the single standing wall still held the thick-roofed houses in a loose embrace. In more modern history (this was a few years before the Japanese Occupation) it had again proved useful against the Hakka foe who on the contemporary occasion had contented themselves with a purely ritual defiance, hurling threats and pulpy, unsavoury missiles over the wall. Both sides had behaved as if the wall were solid masonry, carefully ignoring the existence of the holes. The only safe place during the lobbed bombardment had, in fact, been before the apertures.

The latest immigrants to the settlement had come by ferry. The railway ended in a small market town some miles short of the village. Hoping to confuse possible pursuers, Wallace had decided to disembark at the ferry's penultimate stop; although even the last left a three-hour walk along the deserted sand beaches of this remote coast.

The stubby paddle-steamer had been full of coolies, plastered against the sides of wide-slated lorries, on their way to the new highway that was being driven from an isolated jetty in a circle back to the city. As the ferry glided into the shallow bay over the rubble clearly visible on the bottom, a gong had clanged, echoing hollowly over the water. Far above the gaggle of sheds on the beach a grey and orange geyser had streaked into the void, blossoming at its summit. The crash reached Wallace as the debris bounced off the hillside, crushing trees and bushes in its path. The whiff of cordite drifted over the water. Wallace had been watching with a professional interest, pointing details out to May Ling. She had laughed defiantly: 'It was only a little bang!' Then, as a hooter sounded, the coolies had driven down the gang-plank, the scratching ignitions of their lorries taking one by one.

At the next stop, there were stares as they disembarked. The village formerly served by the stop had long been depopulated and abandoned. The settlement was now used by the army as a firing range. Wallace looked dubiously at the black skull-and-crossbones signs on the wharf, but swung Fong's cardboard case over the side with more decision than he felt. A tanned sailor held May Ling's wrist as she dropped awkwardly onto the planks.

They watched the steamer and its broadside of inquisitive faces skew away. The wheels churned, seeming to get a grip on the unresisting water; then the boat picked up speed, leaving two white rods in its wake.

from *The Monkey King*
by Timothy Mo

Glossary

li an ancient Chinese unit of measurement
geomancer someone who interprets future events by looking at landscape features

Read on!

1   What detail makes you aware that you are reading about the 'real' China?

2   How do you think the writer feels about the place he is describing? Find words or phrases to fill the boxes:

Admiring?	Sarcastic?	Witty?	Hostile?

3   What impression of the village do you think he is trying to create by making the description of the journey so long?

4   Note some of the historical information provided by the author and discuss why he spends so much time on this.

5   How does knowing the historical context add to a 'sense of place'?

6   Wallace Nolasco knows he has to live there. How might this influence his attitude towards the description of the place?

Write on!

1   'A mountain protected the village' is an example of personification. Choose a different kind of landscape, for example, a seascape or a desert. Think of some other examples of personification to make the place more alive.

Feature	Personification	Impression given
Mountain	Protected the village	Comforting – like a guardian or a parent

2   List any other images in the passage which help you to 'see' the place and which strike you as imaginative: for example, consider the metaphors used to describe the roads in the third paragraph. Metaphors firmly state that something 'is' something else.

3   Write about this place.

Over to you!

The vivid picture of the village in the extract is created by:

* accurate and interesting detail;
* imaginative ways of describing the obvious or dull.

Use the structure of the passage and collect detail to write about a place which you know well. Your challenge is to make something which seems uninteresting to you seem interesting and vivid to your reader. Use the Activity Sheet to help.

* Write about the place in order to describe it to someone who has not seen it before. This means you cannot take it for granted that your audience will understand and react to the same things you do.
* Use comparisons and images, such as personification, to make the picture clear.

4 An unusual event

The author describes the earthquake of 1953 on the Greek island of Cephallonia.

There was a thin haze, and streaky clouds like vapour trails were draped across the skies at insouciant angles, as though placed there by an expressionist artist with an allergy to order and serious aesthetic objections to symmetry and form. Drosoula had noticed that there was an inexplicably strange smell and glow upon the land, and Pelagia had found that the water was right up to the top level of the well, even though there had been no rain. Yet minutes later she had returned with her pail and found no liquid there at all. Dr Iannis, who had been tightening the miniature screws of his spectacles, found to his amazement that they stuck to his screwdriver with implausible magnetic force. Antonia, now eight years old but as tall as a child of twelve, went to pick up a sheet of paper from the floor, and the sheet fluttered upwards and stuck to her hand. 'I'm a witch, I'm a witch,' she cried, skipping out of the door, only to find that a hedgehog with two babies was scuttling across the yard, and that a similarly nocturnal owl was inspecting her from a lower branch of the olive, flanked by rows of Pelagia's new chickens that sat roosting obliviously with their heads beneath their wings. If Antonia had looked, she would have seen not one bird flying in the sky, and if she had gone down to the sea, she would have seen flatfish swimming near the surface, and the other fish leaping as if they now wished to be birds and to swim in air, whilst many others preemptively turned turtle, and died.

Snakes and rats left their holes, and the martens in the Cephallonian pines gathered together in groups upon the ground and sat waiting like opera-lovers before the overture begins. Outside the doctor's house a mule tethered to the wall strained against its rope and kicked out at the stones, the thudding of its hooves reverberating in the house. The dogs of the village set up the same ungainly and enervating chorus that normally occurs at dusk, and rivers of crickets streamed purposefully across roads and yards to vanish amongst the thorns. Curious events followed one upon another. Crockery rattled and cutlery clattered just as it had in the war

An unusual event

when British bombers overflew. Outside in the yard Pelagia's bucket fell over, spilling its water, and Antonia denied upsetting it. Drosoula came inside, perspiring and shaking, and told Pelagia, 'I am ill, I feel terrible, something has happened to my heart.' She sat down heavily, clutching her hand to her chest, gasping with anxiety. She had never felt so weak in the limbs, so tormented by pins and needles in the feet. Not since the last feast of the saint had she so much wanted to be sick. She took deep breaths, and Pelagia made her a restorative tisane. Outside in the yard Antonia realised that she was suffering from a headache, was a little giddy, and was also oppressed by that vertiginous terror that one experiences when looking over a precipice and fears that one is being drawn over it. Pelagia came out and said, 'Psipsina, come in and watch; the other Psipsina's going bonkers.' It was true. The cat was indulging in behaviour more mysterious than any seen in any feline since the time of Cleopatra and the Ptolemies. She scratched at the floor as though burying something or unearthing it, and then rolled upon the spot as though expressing pleasure or wriggling against the pricking of her fleas. She skipped suddenly sideways, and then straight up in the air to an extraordinary height. She turned her gaze on the humans for one split second, somersaulted with a wide-eyed expression that could only have meant astonishment, and then shot out of the door and up the tree, where she ignored the chickens. A moment later she was back in the house looking for things to get into. She tried a wicker basket for size, put her head

and forepaws into a brown paper bag, sat for a minute in a pan that was too small to contain her, and ran straight up the wall to perch, blinking owlishly, upon the top of a shutter that was swaying precariously from side to side and creaking with her weight. 'Mad cat,' remonstrated Pelagia, whereupon the animal leapt and skittered from one shelf to another, hurling itself dementedly round and round the room without once touching the floor, in a manner that reminded Pelagia of the cat's eponymous predecessor. She stopped abruptly, her tail fluffed out to splendid dimensions, the hair of her arching back standing straight on end, and she hissed fiercely at an invisible enemy that appeared to be somewhere in the region of the door. Then quietly she returned to the ground, slunk out into the yard as though stalking, and sat on the wall yowling tragically as though perplexed at the loss of kittens or lamenting an atrocity. Antonia, who had been clapping her hands and laughing with delight, suddenly burst into tears, exclaimed, 'Mama, I've got to get out,' and ran outdoors.

Drosoula and Pelagia exchanged glances, as if to say, 'She must have reached puberty early,' when there erupted from the earth below a stupefying roar so far below an audible pitch that it was sensed rather than heard. The two women felt their chests heave and vibrate against the restraint of sinews and cartilage, their ribs seemed to be tearing, a god seeming to be dealing mighty blows to a bass drum within their lungs. 'A heart attack,' thought Pelagia desperately, 'O God, I've never lived,' and she saw Drosoula with her hands to her stomach and her eyes bulging, stumbling towards her as though felled by an axe.

It seemed as though time stopped and the unspeakable growling of the earth would never end. Dr Iannis plunged out of the doorway of the room that used to be Pelagia's and spoke for the first time in eight years: 'Get out! Get out!' he cried, 'It's an earthquake! Save yourselves!' His voice

sounded tinny and infinitely remote behind that guttural explosion of ever-augmenting sound, and he was thrown violently sideways.

Panicked and blinded by the frantic leaping and quivering of the world, the two women lurched for the door, were hurled down, and attempted to crawl. To the infernal and brain-splitting booming of the earth was added the cacophony of cascading pans and dishes, the menacing, wild, but mincing tarantella of chairs and table, the gunshot reports of snapping beams and walls, the random clanging of the church-bell, and a choking cloud of dust with the stench of sulphur that tore at the throat and eyes. They could not crawl on hands and knees for being thrown upwards and sideways, again and again, and they spread their hands and legs and writhed like serpents for the door, reaching it only as the roof began to cave.

Out into the heaving yard they went, the light obliterated from the sky, the direful clamour bursting inside their heads and breasts, dust rising slowly from the earth as though attracted by the moon. The ancient olive, before their very eyes, made obeisance to the ground and split cleanly down the centre of the trunk before springing upright and shaking its branches like a palsied Nazarene. A bubbling and filthy waterspout erupted from the centre of the Street to a height of twelve metres, and then disappeared as though it had never been, leaving a pool of water that filled rapidly with dust and also disappeared. Higher up the hill, invisible because of the ascending curtains of pale and choking dust, a plate of rock and red clay split from the slope and tobogganed down, entering the road to the south side, dragging the olives in its route, and removing the field from which the crickets had migrated. Once more the unsettled giant in the bowels of the earth slammed a mighty fist vertically upwards, so that houses leapt from their foundations and solid stone walls rippled like paper in the wind, and suddenly there was a stillness like that of death. An uncanny and sepulchral silence settled upon the land, as though belatedly regretting such catastrophe, and Pelagia, hawking and filthy, filled beyond measure by a sense of impotence and tininess, began to struggle to her knees, still winded beyond measure by the last titanic blow that had struck her in the diaphragm and paralysed her lungs.

from *Captain Corelli's Mandolin*
by Louis de Bernières

Read on!

1 How can a writer solve the problem of giving his or her audience a sense of such a terrible event when most of the readers of the piece will never have experienced anything like it?

2 What is the purpose of describing such an event in a novel? How can such an event impact upon the story and the characters?

3 How is this different from describing an earthquake in geography?

4 List the details given before the earthquake which give the reader a sense that something unusual is happening.

Physical events	
Actions and reactions of animals	
Actions and reactions of humans	

5 How does the author give you a sense of what it is like during an earthquake?

6 What is the world like after the event? What does it look like? How do the characters react?

Impact on senses	
Physical changes in the earth's surface	

Write on!

1 The plan of the writing in this passage is simple: before, during, after. Imagine you are in school when an earthquake occurs. Follow the plan and the kind of detail you have extracted from the passage in the earlier section. Write about the experience. The Activity Sheet will help.

• Remember, this is not a description in a geographical text (as in Unit 19). Its purpose is to describe what it is like in *personal* terms.

2 Use the details from the passage to write Drosoula's diary extract for the event. Here the audience and purpose are different, but the details will be the same. Use the chart to help.

Purpose of the diary	
Its audience	
Things I would miss out and why	
Things I would add and why	

Over to you!

Using the material in the passage and the approaches you have considered, write a short piece on the 1953 Cephallonian earthquake:

a) as it might appear in a geography book
b) as it might be reported on the TV news
c) as it might appear in a newspaper.

• Use detail from the passage and the comments of characters.

• Decide on the audience and purpose of each piece.

• Which features of style will you have to change in each of the three pieces to match them appropriately to their audience and purpose?

• Compare the three pieces with the original extract. Which do you prefer and why?

5 Describing a place

This text is adapted from a booklet produced by the Corporation of London Public Relations Office about the 1990s refurbishment of Smithfield Market, which was originally opened in 1868 on the site of an ancient meat market.

Before: How it worked

Smithfield's principal buildings – the East and West markets – are separated by Grand Avenue. At right angles to it, Buyers' Walk runs through both markets. Each of the four sections created by these two thoroughfares was, in turn, subdivided by three avenues, creating blocks of stalls.

This arrangement made the markets highly accessible. Not only could meat and market people come and go as they pleased, but so could birds, tourists, motor vehicles (Grand Avenue was, and remains, a public highway) and whatever else the wind might blow in.

By the standards of the mid-nineteenth century, the original building had great merits; the louvered roof, for example, kept summer temperatures lower inside than shade temperatures outside. But late twentieth-century standards demanded more precise regulation of atmosphere, cleanliness and temperature, which was impossible to achieve in the buildings as they stood.

Trucks used to draw up at the gates around the buildings. Then teams of men known as 'pullers back' clambered inside each truck and dragged the carcasses hung up on roof-rails back towards the rear of the truck, positioning each carcass so that it could be dropped down to the next link in the chain. This was another gang of men, known as 'pitchers'. They lifted the carcass on to their shoulders or loaded it on to a handcart and carried or pushed it round to the shop which had ordered it. There the carcass would be pitched up on to another hook.

Once the meat was unloaded and delivered, the next phase was down to the men who worked in the

shops – the 'shopmen'. They weighed and checked the meat, cut the carcasses into smaller pieces (ready to be cut into smaller pieces yet by retail butchers) and laid out or hung the produce for customers to inspect. The shopmen also kept a wary eye on their displays through the night. The Market's easy accessibility was a security nightmare and meat which came in legitimately was all too likely to leave the opposite way.

After: Fit for the future

From the outside the refurbished East market looks much the same as it always has, except that it is cleaner, neater, and freshly painted. But clues that the system has changed are visible. A new canopy of tubular steel and toughened glass runs round the building, much smarter than the old one which was first introduced to protect meat being carried into the market at ground level when transport to the Market by rail gave way to road.

Describing a place

More strikingly different to the new canopy are the two rectangular structures on the north side of the building. These are sealed loading bays. Instead of trucks pulling up at any available gate alongside the building, they now reverse into one of these bays. As soon as a truck is in position in the bay an inflatable seal closes round its rear. The seal will fit any regular-sized truck so tightly that after the truck's tail is opened inside the delivery bay the meat can be unloaded hygienically.

Carcasses are shifted down the truck to the rear as they were before. But instead of being dropped down to a 'pitcher' on the street below they are transferred to hooks on a moving line high above the ground. If a carcass is too heavy to be manhandled a robotic arm transfers it to the line. The carcass now sets off along a rail system, travelling down a new service corridor (which runs the length of the building and is temperature-controlled at 12˚C) until it is diverted along a side rail into a trader's shop or stall.

These new stalls are very different to the old ones. Instead of being open to the air they are, in effect, giant, sealed refrigerated boxes made out of glass and steel – materials used extensively throughout the Market's refurbishment because they are easy to wash down and keep clean. Each stall is divided into sections as required: for cutting and packing, for keeping meat frozen or chilled and for display.

Carcass stalls have display areas at the front; behind them is a chiller room where the carcasses are hung up. Behind the chiller room is a cutting and packing area and behind that a box chiller where meat is kept wrapped and boxed. The refrigeration equipment keeps all the meat at the temperatures required by legislation: red meat at 7˚C; offal at 3˚C; white meat at 4˚C. Whatever the shop's speciality, it is crucially important that every section is rigorously temperature-controlled.

Display areas at the front of every stall open on to the old Buyers' Walk which now divides the Market more simply than before into just two rows of stalls. Customers still parade along the Walk, choosing from the goods on show. But customers, too, have had to change their habits: if they want to go behind the

Buyers' Walk today

display areas to see the meat they must put on white coats and headgear.

What the new layout and equipment have triumphantly achieved is a smooth flow of meat through the Market, from delivery truck to customers' transport, in which produce is at all times kept at the right temperature, and protected from contamination by the constant cleaning of all surfaces and the maintenance of an environment insulated from the outside world.

The people who work there have joined a new flow of their own; it merges seamlessly with the hygiene arrangements which have been built into the physical fabric of the Market. No longer do workers turn up at any entrance and change wherever they please – usually in a small room up a narrow spiral staircase above a trader's shop. Now they must go through a strict process in a new communal welfare section built on the floor above the Market. There they change into all-white protective clothing, from the mandatory hard hats down to the non-slip boots. In the Market below, there are rooms where they can wash their hands and scrub their boots as they move to and from their stalls. Cleaning is the focus around which human and physical requirements mesh most closely to let the new regime work to a high peak of effectiveness.

from *Smithfield: A Market for Our Time* by Stephen Fay and Eric Jacobs

Read on!

1 What was the main reason for altering the Market?

Support your answers by quoting from the text.

2 What does this passage tell you about the original features of Smithfield Market, kept during the refurbishment?

3 List the main changes described in this passage. Consider access for customers and the general public, the running of the Market and people's work.

4 What does the passage say are the benefits of the changes?

5 Which of these benefits does it stress?

6 What impression is the passage trying to give of the Market?

Write on!

1 This descriptive passage is also presenting an argument to convince the reader that the refurbishment of the Market was carried out for a good reason.

- List short extracts which suggest that the description is also an argument.
- Underline the key words.
- Comment on the extracts.

Word, phrase or sentence	Comment
'Not only could meat and market people come and go as they pleased, but so could birds, tourists and whatever else the wind blew in.'	Access to the market needed to be controlled.

2 The passage emphasises the Corporation's sensitivity towards the conservation of the building and its traditions.

- List short extracts which contribute to this impression.
- Underline the key words.
- Comment on the extracts.

3 What impression is created of the refurbished market by the following words and phrases:

a) neater, freshly painted, smarter

b) cleaner, hygienically, sealed, temperature-controlled

c) smooth flow, merges seamlessly

d) rigorously, strict, regime.

To each of the above lists add any other words which create the same impression.

Over to you!

1 Describe a place which you think needs to be refurbished. Include the good points to keep and any to change. Say why these changes should be made. The Activity Sheet will help you.

2 List the benefits of the refurbishment.

Make a note of words you can use to stress these benefits.

3 Describe the place after the changes.

- Show how the changes have conserved the traditions and the appearance of the place.
- Emphasise the necessity of the changes and the improvements they have made.

Use language which emphasises the ways in which traditions and appearance have been conserved.

6 Advertising

The Advertising Standards Authority (ASA) supervises the rules laid out in the British Codes of Advertising and Sales Promotion. These are the rules which the industry has written and agreed to follow.

Advertising Standards Authority

"Advertising Under Control"

ASA

- Self Regulation
- News
- Adjudications
- Issues
- ☑ The Codes
- Annual Report
- Research
- Successes
- Links
- Keep me informed
- How to complain
- Contact Us
- Search

The Codes

Alcoholic drinks

The rules

The consumption of alcohol may be portrayed as sociable and thirst-quenching but advertisers must avoid encouraging or portraying styles of drinking which are unwise for drinkers. For example, neither excessive nor solitary drinking should be encouraged. Specific rules include:

Young people: Advertisements for alcoholic drinks should not be directed at the under-18s through the medium used, the style of presentation, or the context in which they appear. No medium should be used to advertise alcoholic drinks if more than 25% of its audience is under 18.

Safety: Alcohol must not be linked with any activity or location where consumption would be unsafe or unwise. In particular, consumption should not be associated with anything which requires concentration to be done safely, such as driving, operating machinery or activity relating to water or heights. For low-alcohol drinks there should be no suggestion that there is a 'safe' level of consumption.

Social success: Advertisements should not suggest that a drink will enhance masculinity or femininity or lead to social, sporting or sexual success. Alcohol should not be portrayed as the main reason for the success of a party or event.

Alcohol content: While it is legitimate to give factual information about the alcoholic strength of a brand, it is not acceptable to use high alcohol-content as the basis of any appeal. Brands should not be advertised in the form of a challenge to drinkers.

Humour: Advertisements may be humorous but must still conform with the intention of the rules.

Complaints

In 2000, the ASA resolved 12,389 complaints, of which 166 were about advertisements for alcoholic drinks. This compared to a total of 12,141 complaints resolved in 1999, of which 155 were about alcoholic drinks.

ASA research

Since 1988, the ASA has kept a special watch on alcohol advertisements. Many advertisers and agencies in this sector also seek advice from the industry's Copy Advice team at pre-publication stage. The problems are minimal because advertisers take care to sort out difficulties before they proceed to publication.

ASA research into alcoholic drinks advertising in the summer of 1996 revealed that less than 2% raised problems under the Codes. From a sample of 359 advertisements for alcoholic drinks drawn from national newspapers and a selection of regional, consumer and trade publications, only four raised problems under the Codes. Two appeared to encourage or condone excessive consumption through multi-buy promotions for an off-licence, one used the alcoholic strength of the drink as the main advertising platform, and one featured a model who appeared to be under 25.

Alcopops

There were 12 advertisements in the sample for alcoholic carbonates (alcopops), all but two of which appeared in the trade press. None broke the Codes.

The ASA carried out a follow-up check in October 1996, finding only three advertisements for alcopops, none of which broke the Codes.

from the website of the Advertising Standards Authority: http://www.asa.org.uk.
(The British Codes of Advertising and Sales Promotion are now in their 10th edition. They are written by a Committee of Advertising Practice [www.cap.org.uk], which is made up of 19 trade bodies representing the whole of the UK advertising industry.)

Read on!

1. What is the aim of an advertisement?
2. List the variety of media in which people advertise. In what ways can products be advertised in each?

TV and film	Moving visuals, sound
Magazines	Still pictures, words
Internet	

3. In what ways could advertisements be dangerous to their audiences?

4. Why is there a need for the Advertising Standards Authority?
5. In the passage, what do the changes in the complaints figures suggest?
6. Why does 'Alcopops' need a special section to itself?
7. Summarise the rules from the passage:

Young people	Safety	Social success	Alcohol content	Humour

8. Do you disagree with any of these? Why?

Write on!

1. Write the script for an advertisement for a new brand of 'Alcopops' which breaks all the rules stated here.

   - For which medium are you producing an advertisement?
   - Is it visual or words only?
   - How can visuals alone communicate some of the rules above?

2. a) Exchange your work with a partner and criticise one another's advertisements on the basis of the ASA rules.
   b) Rewrite the advertisement so that it is 'amended' and not 'withdrawn'.

3. Write a similar set of rules which could apply to advertising hair and beauty products or mobile phones.

   - Consider all the advertisements of those products which you know and analyse whom they are trying to influence.
   - What do you consider the most important factors to take into consideration when dealing with those products?
   - What dangers could there be if there were no rules for them?

Over to you!

Research shows that certain tactics are used in advertisements aimed at young people, whether or not the rules of the ASA are considered. The message is that if you buy certain products you are assured of certain features.

1. Complete a chart with examples of advertisements you have seen, saying whether you think they are ethical or not. The Activity Sheet will help.

2. Use these data to create the content of a newspaper article explaining the work of the ASA and pointing out the dangers of unethical advertising for young people. Describe the need for the ASA.

   - Use examples from your research and this unit to show how young people may be influenced to spend their money unwisely.

7 Describing a person

This passage is from a book written by a doctor and is based on case studies of patients.

Rebecca

Rebecca was no child when she was referred to our clinic. She was nineteen but, as her grandmother said, 'just like a child in some ways'. She could not find her way around the block, she could not confidently open a door with a key (she could never 'see' how the key went, and never seemed to learn). She had left/right confusion, she sometimes put on her clothes the wrong way – inside out, back-to-front – without appearing to notice, or, if she noticed, without being able to get them right. She might spend hours jamming a hand or foot into the wrong glove or shoe – she seemed, as her grandmother said, to have 'no sense of space'. She was clumsy and ill-coordinated in all her movements – 'a 'klutz', one report said, a 'motor moron' another (although when she danced, all her clumsiness disappeared).

Rebecca had a partially cleft palate, which caused a whistling in her speech; short, stumpy fingers, with blunt, deformed nails; and a high, degenerative myopia requiring very thick spectacles – all stigmata of the same congenital condition which had caused her cerebral and mental defects. She was painfully shy and withdrawn, feeling that she was, and had always been, a figure of fun.

But she was capable of warm, deep, even passionate attachments. She had a deep love for her grandmother, who had brought her up since she was three. She was very fond of nature and, if she were taken to the city parks and botanic gardens, spent many happy hours there. She was very fond, too, of stories, although she never learned to read (despite assiduous, and even frantic, attempts) and would implore her grandmother or others to read to her. Fortunately her grandmother loved reading stories and had a fine reading voice which kept Rebecca entranced. And not just stories – poetry too. This seemed a deep need or hunger in Rebecca – a necessary form of nourishment, of reality, for her mind. Nature was beautiful, but mute. It was not enough. She needed the world re-presented to her in verbal images, in language, and seemed to have little difficulty following the metaphors and symbols of even quite deep poems, in striking contrast to her incapacity with simple propositions and instructions. The language of feeling, of the concrete, of image and symbol formed a world she loved and, to a remarkable extent, could enter.

When I first saw her – clumsy, uncouth, all-of-a-fumble – I saw her merely, or wholly, as a casualty, a broken creature, whose neurological impairments I could pick out and dissect with precision: a multitude of apraxias and agnosias, a mass of sensorimotor impairments and breakdowns, limitations of intellectual schemata and concepts similar to those (by Piaget's criteria) of a child of eight. A poor thing, I said to myself, with perhaps a 'splinter skill', a freak gift, of speech.

The next time I saw her, it was all very different. I didn't have her in a test situation, 'evaluating' her in a clinic. I wandered outside, it was a lovely day, with a few minutes in hand before the clinic started, and there I saw Rebecca sitting on a bench, gazing at the April foliage quietly, with obvious delight. Her posture had none of the clumsiness which had so impressed me before. Sitting there, in a light dress, her face calm and slightly smiling, she suddenly brought to mind one of Chekov's young women seen against the backdrop of a cherry orchard. She could have been any young woman enjoying a beautiful spring day. This was my human, as opposed to my neurological, vision.

As I approached she heard my footsteps and turned, gave me a broad smile, and wordlessly gestured. 'Look at the world,' she seemed to say. 'How beautiful it is.' And then there came out, in spurts, odd, sudden, poetic ejaculations: 'spring', 'birth', 'growing', 'stirring', 'coming to life', 'seasons', 'everything in its time'. I found myself thinking of Ecclesiastes: 'To everything there is a season, and a time to every purpose under the heaven. A time to be born, and a time to die; a time to plant, and a time …' This was what Rebecca, in her disjointed fashion, was ejaculating – a vision of seasons, of times, like that of the Preacher. She had done appallingly in the testing – which, in a sense, was designed, like all neurological and psychological testing, not merely to uncover, to bring out deficits, but to decompose her into functions and deficits. She had come apart, horribly, in formal testing, but now she was mysteriously 'together' and composed.

Why was she so de-composed before, how could she be so re-composed now? I had the strongest feeling of two wholly different modes of thought, or of organisation, or of being. The first schematic – pattern-seeing, problem-solving – this is what had been tested, and where she had been found so defective, so disastrously wanting. But the tests had given no inkling of anything *but* the defects, anything, so to speak, *beyond* her defects.

They had given me no hint of her positive powers, her ability to perceive the real world – the world of nature, and perhaps of the imagination – as a coherent, intelligible, poetic whole; her ability to see this, and (where she could) live this; they had given me no intimation of her inner world, which clearly *was* composed and coherent, and approached as something other than a set of problems or tasks.

It was perhaps fortunate that I chanced to see Rebecca in her so-different modes – so damaged and incorrigible in the one, so full of promise and potential in the other – and that she was one of the first patients I saw in our clinic. For what I saw in her, what she showed me, I now saw in them all.

from *The Man Who Mistook His Wife for a Hat* by Oliver Sacks

Glossary

agnosia Inability to recognise objects by one of the senses
apraxia Inability to carry out actions, as a result of brain disorder
klutz A stupid, clumsy, socially-inept person
Piaget Jean Piaget (1896–1980), pioneer in the study of children's intellectual development
schemata (plural) Unconscious mental models which help a person to make sense of new information
sensorimotor Concerning activities which involve the functions of the senses and actions

Read on!

1   What first impression do the following words and phrases give of Rebecca?

2
Word or phrase	Impression
confusion	
jamming	
ill-coordinated	
moron	

From the first two paragraphs, what is your impression of Rebecca?

3   How does the writer prepare the reader, in the first paragraph, for the discovery of Rebecca's hidden abilities?

4   By the end of the third paragraph, how has the writer's (and your own) impression of Rebecca changed?

5   Which words and phrases from the first four paragraphs give the impression that the writer held little hope for Rebecca's future development?

6   In the description of the second time the writer saw Rebecca, which words emphasise her sense of harmony and peace?
Contrast these with the words used in connection with his first meeting with her.

7   The writer contrasts his 'human' with his 'neurological' vision (his later response to Rebecca, as a human being, with his earlier response as a neurologist). How are these two responses expressed in his choice of words?

Write on!

1   Imagine (or remember) your first meeting with someone whose imperfections are the main things you notice.

   a)   Make notes about the person's imperfections, and list words to refer to them which express the impression you have of the person. The Activity Sheet will help you.

   b)   List some of the things the person says or does, again using words which express the impression you have of the person. Example from the passage: 'jamming a hand or foot into the wrong glove or shoe' conveys the impression of clumsiness.

2   Imagine (or remember) a later meeting with the same person, when you begin to find out more about him or her and your first impression begins to change.

   Make notes about what the person says or does and what they reveal to you about him or her.

Over to you!

The doctor who wrote the passage describes how the settings in which he met Rebecca affected her behaviour and so affected his impressions of her.

Using your notes from questions 1 and 2 above, describe your two meetings with the same person, showing how the setting affected his or her behaviour.

Use words which help to convey this impression.

8 A diary (fiction)

Thursday January 1st   **BANK HOLIDAY IN ENGLAND, IRELAND, SCOTLAND & WALES**

These are my New Year's resolutions:

1. I will help the blind across the road.

2. I will hang my trousers up.

3. I will put the sleeves back on my records.

4. I will not start smoking.

5. I will stop squeezing my spots.

6. I will be kind to the dog.

7. I will help the poor and ignorant.

8. After hearing the disgusting noises from downstairs last night, I have also vowed never to drink alcohol.

My father got the dog drunk on cherry brandy at the party last night. If the RSPCA hear about it he could get done. Eight days have gone by since Christmas Day but my mother still hasn't worn the green lurex apron I bought her for Christmas! She will get bathcubes next year.

  Just my luck, I've got a spot on my chin for the first day of the New Year!

Friday January 2nd   **BANK HOLIDAY IN SCOTLAND. FULL MOON**

I felt rotten today. It's my mother's fault for singing 'My Way' at two o'clock in the morning at the top of the stairs. Just my luck to have a mother like her. There is a chance my parents could be alcoholics. Next year I could be in a children's home.

  The dog got its own back on my father. It jumped up and knocked down his model ship, then ran into the garden with the rigging tangled in its feet. My father kept saying, 'Three months' work down the drain', over and over again.

  The spot on my chin is getting bigger. It's my mother's fault for not knowing about vitamins.

Saturday January 3rd

I shall go mad through lack of sleep! My father has banned the dog from the house so it barked outside my window all night. Just my luck! My father shouted a swear-word at it.

  If he's not careful he will get done by the police for obscene language.

  I think the spot is a boil. Just my luck to have it where everybody can see it. I pointed out to my mother that I hadn't had any vitamin C today. She said, 'Go and buy an orange, then'. This is typical.

  She still hasn't worn the lurex apron.

  I will be glad to get back to school.

Sunday January 4th   **SECOND AFTER CHRISTMAS**

My father has got the flu. I'm not surprised with the diet we get. My mother went out in the rain to get him a vitamin C drink, but as I told her, 'It's too late now'. It's a miracle we don't get scurvy. My mother says she can't see anything on my chin, but this is guilt because of the diet.

A diary (fiction)

The dog has run off because my mother didn't close the gate. I have broken the arm on the stereo. Nobody knows yet, and with a bit of luck my father will be ill for a long time. He is the only one who uses it apart from me. No sign of the apron.

Monday January 5th

The dog hasn't come back yet. It is peaceful without it. My mother rang the police and gave a description of the dog. She made it sound worse than it actually is: straggly hair over its eyes and all that. I really think the police have got better things to do than look for dogs, such as catching murderers. I told my mother this but she still rang them. Serve her right if she was murdered because of the dog. My father is still lazing about in bed. He is supposed to be ill, but I noticed he is still smoking!

Nigel came round today. He has got a tan from his Christmas holiday. I think Nigel will be ill soon from the shock of the cold in England. I think Nigel's parents were wrong to take him abroad.

He hasn't got a single spot yet.

Tuesday January 6th   **EPIPHANY. NEW MOON**

The dog is in trouble!

It knocked a meter-reader off his bike and messed all the cards up. So now we will all end up in court I expect. A policeman said we must keep the dog under control and asked how long it had been lame. My mother said it wasn't lame, and examined it. There was a tiny model pirate trapped in its left front paw.

The dog was pleased when my mother took the pirate out and it jumped up the policeman's tunic with its muddy paws. My mother fetched a cloth from the kitchen but it had strawberry jam on it where I had wiped the knife, so the tunic was worse than ever. The policeman went then. I'm sure he swore. I could report him for that.

I will look up 'Epiphany' in my new dictionary.

Wednesday January 7th

Nigel came round on his new bike this morning. It has got a water bottle, a milometer, a speedometer, a yellow saddle, and very thin racing wheels. It's wasted on Nigel. He only goes to the shops and back on it. If I had it, I would go all over the country and have an experience.

My spot or boil has reached its peak. Surely it can't get any bigger!

I found a word in my dictionary that describes my father.

It is 'malingerer'. He is still in bed guzzling vitamin C.

The dog is locked in the coal shed.

Epiphany is something to do with the three wise men. Big deal!

from *The Secret Diary of Adrian Mole Aged 13¾* by Sue Townsend

Read on!

1   What features do you notice about a diary which make it different from other texts? List them and comment on their use.

Layout	Written in sections – small amounts are acceptable
Length of sentences	

2   How do these features help to establish the purpose of this kind of writing?

3   Identify any personal pronouns in the first entry. What do you notice? How would these probably be different from telling the same story in a novel?

4   a)   Identify the verbs and their tenses in various diary entries. Which tense is most used?

   b)   How might this show how a diary reflects almost 'talking' directly to your audience?

5   Which parts of the Adrian Mole passage do you find most amusing?

Write on!

1   Identify the features of this diary. The Activity Sheet will help.

Feature	Comment and examples in the passage
Tense used	
Length of sentences	

2   Continue with Adrian Mole's diary in an appropriate style for another few days, but make it more serious as he returns to school.

   • Continue with the stories of the dog, his father's illness, his mother's refusal to wear his Christmas present and his resentment of Nigel.

   • How is the tone of your text different from the original? Which do you prefer and why?

Over to you!

Write some extracts from a humorous diary about life in your home over a holiday or at a festival time.

   • What details are important to consider?
   • What do you consider amusing or absurd enough to mention?
   • Do you only concentrate on things which annoy you, because a diary is a personal document?

   • Consider people's actions and reactions when the family is all together for such a long time.
   • Decide for whom you are really writing and how this influences the way you write.

Remember to use the stylistic features of the diary form. The Activity Sheet will help.

9 A diary (non-fiction)

These extracts are from the diary of a young man from East Cumbria. When he died, in the 1950s, his relatives cleared his house and piled up in the garden any of his possessions which they did not want. Among the 'rubbish' was a small tin box. A passer-by opened the box, which contained the diary, a photograph and a few other personal items. He kept the diary for forty years before it was published (the identity of the young miner was not revealed). The spelling and upper- and lower-case letters are as they were in the original, but sometimes full stops have been added or removed to help you to make sense of the diary.

1907

Thursday 3rd January

fine day. frosty moon Light at 8pm. Tom Armstrong & Joseph Monkhouse up with Graphone belonging to Tom Armstrong of Little House Crossgates Lime works.

Sunday 6th January

fine but a thaw. I at Brampton town in the evening but not with any girls at all. talking to James Grant George Grants son of HBGate. I believe H. Arm is at Carlisle not going any more with her.

Friday 18th January

Splendid day sun shining a slight frost in the evening. Thomas Foster Curdiff leading John Parks Tom Routledge & Dick Potts and Tom Brown's manure out on to meadow. Greenhouse fire going on splendid. Greenhouse often up to 60 degrees in heat.

Saturday 19th January

Path Saturday. Pit working. Uncle Joe Routledge down and his son Fred. we were putting mangle together. I went off to Brampton about 6 p.m. with a pair of sconded clogs that did not fit. I Left Brampton about 20 mins past 8. came most of the way with W. Nixon tailor of Milton. Not with any girls at all. and from Farlam Hall with R Park and Maggie.

Sunday 20th January

fine day. I at Brampton junction in evening. Fred Potts and Wilsons son of William Gill. as we were going through Birkey Brow there was three girls in before us and we were chaffing them and I got hold of one of them and went to Brampton station with her. her name was Telford of High Close Talkin. I went from Stat. to B. and met H.A. on Sands and we went round by fourgate down past Swarthall Cottages to Brampton. H.A.

Wednesday 23rd January

Very cold wind in east. 3 tubs went up in Cage and stoped Pit a long time 1 hour. George Bell dead Forest Head.

Friday 25th January

Very cold dull like rain or snow but a thaw. frosty in the evening. Robert Teasdale of Waterlow Greenhead killed with full set at the Enjine Plane curve Greenhead pit to night.

Saturday 26th January

fine day but cold. slight snow shower at night. Pay Saturday. I at work. went to start at 4 a.m. was taking Long iron out of Old Horse Level at the top of the first incline. William Grant and I also John Rutherford Haward some part of the shift. we toke it up to the top of far away incline to take in bye. I getting hay in. the afternoon at Bow Bank Wood for leave mould for flowers. Planted Rhubarb in the frame. John down at Brampton. I Landed back from Bowbank wood about 5 and not away after that from Home.

Sunday 27th January

fine till 6.30 then heavy showers of rain. Cousin Fred Routledge and me at Brampton junction but not with any girls of any kind. H.A. at Armstrongs and M Jane Maggie of Doleshole. I did not see her.

Tuesday 29th January

Frosty. Heavy Snow Showers and cold & drifting snow 4 or 6 in depth a foot or more where it is drifted. Otter seen in Cleskets Beck.

The photograph which was found in the tin with the diary. The young man who wrote the diary is standing on the right.

A diary (non-fiction)

Saturday 9th February

Thawing. Pay. 1/- off for Robert Teasdale Greenhead. I at work filling coals up No 11 Joe. H Armstrong Putting of me John Stobbart Braking No 11 dilly I brought a pipe home from Roachburn Pit for stove. At

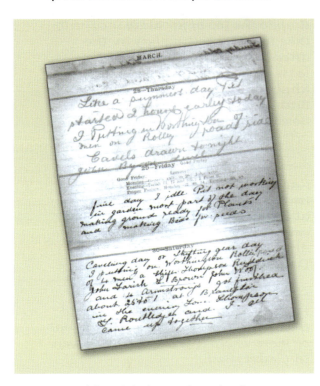

One of the original pages from the diary

HBGate evening with no one. Murrow of Greenwell got Tom Routledge calfe for 55 shillings so they say. Northern Lights flashing all over the sky.

Sunday 10th February

I at Brampton Sands meeting Hannah Armstrong for a walk up Middle road. I had not seen her for 3 Sund nights till Sunday 10th.

Saturday 16th February

Very wet in the evening fine morning high wind at night and rain. I at work. Bath Saturday. putting of the men on Rollyroad side between No 2 and 3 and No 2 Worthington. I toke rose into Greenhouse out of Garden. Tom Routledge cow of to Carlisle auction today.

Sunday 17th February

Sunday evening at Brampton. I was with H.A. up Middle road and down along to Swarthal Cottages tried to go up close near a gate but could not succeed. we partly differed up How-gate as I told her I was coming no more. she was sorry and said that it was not her blame that we differ.

from *A Miner's Diary of 1907*
edited by Alastair Robertson

Glossary [including unconventional spellings]

B Brampton
Cage The cage-like lift in which miners were transported up and down between different levels of the coal mine
Dilly A railway in the pit on which the wagons ran downhill, controlled from the top of the incline by a cable-brake drum or wheel. A cart or wagon was also called a dilly
Enjine [engine] **Plane curve** An underground section of the mine
Graphone [Gramophone] or phonograph
H.A./H. Arm Hannah Armstrong

HBG, HBGate Hallbankgate
In bye Towards the inside of the pit
Level A horizontal passage in a mine
Long iron Long iron rails. A plate-layer used to lay the long iron rails on which the pit wagons ran (and take them up once a coal seam was exhausted)
Path [Bath]
Rollyroad A wagonway or 'tubway' (a railway which carried wagons or 'tubs' of coal from the pit)
Sconded Secondhand
1/- One shilling (5p)

Read on!

1 For what audience is this diary written, and for what purpose? How do these differ from those of the diary in Unit 8?

2 What do you learn from the diary about:

   a) the writer's work?

   b) his wages, when he is paid and how well-off or poor he is?

   c) his clothes and personal hygiene?

   d) his education?

   e) the community in which he lived?

   f) his home life?

   g) his leisure time?

   h) his interests?

   i) his attitude to death?

3 Brampton Junction was a nearby railway station. Why do you think the local youngsters went there so often when they were not catching trains?

4 What are the 'Northern Lights' (Saturday 9 February)?

5 List any other observations of nature:

Date	Observation of nature

Use dictionaries and reference books.

Write on!

1 List the abbreviations used in the diary and explain what they mean.

2 Which words does the writer sometimes spell wrongly (other than by abbreviating them), and how should they be spelled?

   Explain how he has tackled these spellings.

Wrongly-spelled word	Explanation	Correct spelling
graphone	Knows it has 'ph' for 'f' sound. Misses out the syllable 'mo' after 'gra'	gramophone
sconded		

3 Later, the miner writes about the plants he is growing and about an illness he has, and is able to spell words such as 'chrysanthemum' and 'diarrhoea' correctly.

List other difficult words or place-names which he spells correctly (for instance, 'light'). Why do you think he spelled several everyday words wrongly, yet spelled some difficult words correctly?

4 Note any words which are unexpected from a young coal miner, and which he would not use with his friends. Suggest why he might use them in his diary.

5 The writer records only what he did and what went on in his community, making no comment about his feelings. Occasionally, however, you can get an inkling of his feelings from the events he describes. For one of those events, describe the feeling which you can sense, and how.

Over to you!

Re-write the diary for the present-day.

Write only about events, with no comments or expressions of feelings.

Base it on your own experiences but, like this writer, do not include personal details.

Use the Activity Sheet to help you.

Include: the weather, nature; events in the home and family, at school or work and in the community; and what the person did in the evenings and weekends.

10 The structure of a story

As Gregor Samsa awoke one morning from uneasy dreams he found himself transformed in his bed into a gigantic insect. He was lying on his hard, as it were, armour-plated back and when he lifted his head a little he could see his dome-like brown belly divided into stiff arched segments on top of which the bed-quilt could hardly keep in position and was about to slide off completely. His numerous legs, which were pitifully thin compared to the rest of the bulk, waved helplessly before his eyes.

What has happened to me? he thought. It was no dream. His room, a regular human bedroom, only rather too small, lay quiet between the four familiar walls. Above the table on which a collection of cloth samples was unpacked and spread out – Samsa was a commercial traveller – hung the picture which he had recently cut out of an illustrated magazine and put into a pretty gilt frame. It showed a lady, with a fur cap on and a fur stole, sitting upright and holding out to the spectator a huge fur muff into which her forearm had vanished.

Gregor's eyes turned next to the window, and the overcast sky – one could hear raindrops beating on the window gutter – made him feel quite melancholy. What about sleeping a little longer and forgetting all this nonsense, he thought, but it could not be done, for he was accustomed to sleep on his right side and in his present condition he could not turn himself over. However violently he forced himself towards his right side he always rolled on his back again. He tried it at least a hundred times, shutting his eyes to keep from seeing his struggling legs, and only desisted when he began to feel in his side a faint dull ache he had never experienced before.

O God, he thought, what an exhausting job I've picked on! Travelling about day in, day out. It's much more irritating work than doing the actual work in the warehouse, and on top of that there's the trouble of constant travelling, of worrying about train connections, the bed and irregular meals, casual acquaintances that are always new and never become intimate friends. The devil take it all! He felt a slight itching up on his belly; slowly pushed himself on his back nearer to the top of the bed so he could lift his head more easily; identified the itching place which was surrounded by many little white spots the nature of which he could not understand, and made to touch it with a leg, but drew the leg back immediately, for the contact made a cold shiver run through him.

He slid down again into his former position. This getting up early, he thought, makes one quite stupid. A man needs his sleep ... He looked at the alarm-clock ticking on the chest. Heavenly father! he thought. It was half past six o'clock and the hands were quietly moving on, it was even past the half hour, it was getting on for a quarter to seven. Had the alarm-clock not gone off? From the bed one could see that it had been properly set for four o'clock; of course it must have gone off. Yes, but was it possible to sleep quietly though that ear-splitting noise? Well, he had not slept quietly, yet apparently all the more soundly for that. But what was he to do now? The next train went at seven o'clock; to catch that he would need to hurry like mad and his samples weren't even packed up, and he himself wasn't feeling particularly fresh and active. And even if he did catch the train he wouldn't avoid a row with the chief, since the warehouse porter would have been waiting for the five o'clock train and would have long ago reported his failure to turn up. The porter was a creature of the chief's, spineless and stupid. Well, supposing he were to say he was sick? But that would be most unpleasant and would look suspicious, since during his five years' employment he had not been ill once. The chief himself would be sure to come with the sick-insurance doctor, would reproach his parents for their son's laziness, and would cut all excuses short by referring to the insurance doctor, who of course regarded all mankind as perfectly healthy malingerers. And would he be far wrong on this occasion? Gregor really felt quite well, apart from a drowsiness that was utterly superfluous after such a long sleep, and he was even unusually hungry.

All this was running through his mind at top speed without being able to decide to leave his bed – the alarm-clock had just struck a quarter to seven – there came a cautious rap at the door behind the head of his bed. 'Gregor,' said a voice – it was his mother's – 'it's a quarter to seven. Hadn't you a train to catch?' That gentle voice! Gregor had a shock as he heard his own voice answering hers, unmistakably his own voice, it was true, but with a persistent horrible twittering squeak behind it like an undertone, that left the words in their clear shape only for the first moment and then rose up reverberating round them to destroy their sense, so that one could not be sure one had heard them rightly.

from *Metamorphosis*
by Franz Kafka

Read on!

1. Use a dictionary to find the meaning of 'metamorphosis'. Why is it a good title for this story?
2. How do you react to the first sentence? How does it set the tone for what you expect as you read on?
3. Is it a good opening for a story? Why?
4. Find the detail from the extract which makes this impossible situation seem possible.
5. How are the things Gregor thinks about surprising in such a situation?
6. How do you think the story will continue? What happens when his mother sees him? How will she react? What will she say?
7. What sort of ending do you think this story will have? Happy? Sad? Humorous? Gruesome?
8. Explain why 'I woke up. It was all a dream' would be an unsuitable ending to the story.

Write on!

1. This story is famous for its opening. Why is the opening paragraph unusual? Consider:

    - its content
    - its tone
    - how you might have reacted.

2. Using the cut and paste facility of a word-processing package, experiment with opening this story with a different paragraph and then filling in the missing detail. What is the effect of this on the writing style and structure?

3. Stories usually have a simple structure: a statement of the situation, a development of this into a key moment and a resolution. Think of three or four well-known fairy stories or fables and consider their structure. The Activity Sheet will help.

Story	Situation	Development	Resolution
Snow White	Evil stepmother – Snow White runs away – meets seven dwarfs	Poison apple	Rescued by Prince – wicked stepmother defeated

Over to you!

Imagine yourself transformed into something very different. Write about your metamorphosis. Think carefully about how you will open your story.

- How did you react immediately?
- What did you look like?
- How could you move?

- What changes do you notice in your environment – are you smaller or larger? Do things smell or feel differently?
- How do others react to you?

Consider carefully how you will follow the structure outlined earlier in the unit.

11 Playscripts

West Side Story *is a modern musical based on* Romeo and Juliet. *It is set in New York and the two lovers belong to rival gangs: Jets and Sharks – Puerto Ricans and Americans.*

(*The lights fade on the others, who disappear into the haze of the background as a delicate cha-cha begins and Tony and Maria slowly walk forward to meet one another. Slowly, as though in a dream, they drift into the steps of the dance, always looking at one another; completely lost in one another; unaware of anyone, any place, any time, anything but one another.*)

TONY: You're not thinking I'm someone else?

MARIA: I know you are not.

TONY: Or that we have met before?

MARIA: I know we have *not*.

TONY: I felt, I *knew* something-never-before was going to happen, had to happen. But this is –

MARIA (*interrupting*): My hands are cold. (*He takes them in his.*) Yours, too. (*He moves her hands to his face.*) So warm.

(*She moves his hands to her face.*)

TONY: Yours too.

MARIA: But of course. They are the same.

TONY: It's so much to believe – you're not joking me?

MARIA: I have not yet learned how to joke that way. I think now I never will.

(*Impulsively, he stops to kiss her hands; then tenderly, innocently, her lips. The music bursts out, the lights flare up, and Bernardo is upon them in an icy rage.*)

BERNARDO: Go home, 'American'.

TONY: Slow down, Bernardo.

BERNARDO: Stay away from my sister!

TONY: Sister?

(*Riff steps up.*)

BERNARDO (*To Maria*): Couldn't you see he's one of them?

Playscripts

MARIA: No; I saw only him.

BERNARDO (*as Chino comes up*): I told you: there's only one thing they want from a Puerto Rican girl!

TONY: That's a lie!

RIFF: Cool boy.

CHINO (*To Tony*): Get away.

TONY: You keep out, Chino. (*To Maria*) Don't listen to them!

BERNARDO: She will listen to her brother before –

RIFF (*Overlapping*): If you characters want to settle –

GLAD HAND: Please! Everything was going so well! Do you fellows get pleasure out of making trouble? Now come on – it won't hurt you to have a good time.

(*Music starts again. Bernardo is on one side with Maria and Chino; Anita joins them. Tony is on the other with Riff and Diesel. Light emphasises the first group.*)

BERNARDO: I warned you –

CHINO: Do not yell at her, 'Nardo.

BERNARDO: You yell at babies.

ANITA: And put ideas in the baby's head.

BERNARDO: Take her home, Chino.

MARIA: 'Nardo, it is my first dance.

BERNARDO : Please. We are family, Maria. Go.

(*Maria hesitates, then starts out with Chino as the light follows her to the other group, which she passes.*)

RIFF (*To Diesel, indicating Tony happily*): I guess the kid's with us for sure now.

(*Tony doesn't even hear; he is staring at Maria, who stops for a moment.*)

CHINO: Come Maria.

(*They continue out.*)

TONY: Maria …

(*He is unaware that Bernardo is crossing towards him, but Riff intercepts.*)

BERNARDO: I don't want you.

RIFF: I want you though. For a war council – Jets and Sharks.

BERNARDO: The pleasure is mine.

RIFF: Let's go outside.

BERNARDO: I would not leave the ladies alone. We will meet you in half an hour.

RIFF: Doc's drugstore? (*Bernardo nods.*) And no jazz before then.

BERNARDO: I understand the rules – Native Boy.

(*The light is fading on them, on everyone but Tony.*)

RIFF: Spread the word, Diesel.

DIESEL: Right, Daddy-o.

RIFF: Let's get the chicks and kick it. Tony?

TONY: Maria … (*Music starts.*)

RIFF (*In darkness*): Tony!

DIESEL (*In darkness*): Ah, we'll see him at Doc's.

TONY (*Speaking dreamily over the music – he is now standing alone in the light*): Maria.

(*Singing softly*) The most beautiful sound I ever heard.

VOICES *offstage*: Maria, Maria, Maria, Maria …

TONY: All the beautiful sounds of the world in a single word:

VOICES *offstage*: Maria, Maria, Maria, Maria (*Swelling in intensity*) Maria, Maria.

from *West Side Story*
by Arthur Laurents and Stephen Sondheim

Read on!

1. Discuss whether playscripts are written primarily to be read or to be acted.
2. How does this influence the features necessary for a playscript: for example, layout and punctuation?
3. Why is it necessary to have such defined stage directions and instructions to actors in a playscript?
4. How does the author indicate which parts of a playscript are to be spoken?
5. How does a playwright communicate a character's feelings and how he or she reacts? What would the writer of a novel do differently in these circumstances?
6. Read *Romeo and Juliet*, Act I, Scene v. What differences are there between this version of the play and Shakespeare's original? Use the chart to help.

Feature	Romeo and Juliet	West Side Story
Location		
Era		
Reason for tension		
Language used		

Write on!

1. Identify and list the conventions of a playscript in the passage by completing the chart. The Activity Sheet will help.
2. Continue this scene using the same characters, setting and language.

   - Remember to use the dramatic conventions to show how characters are feeling and reacting. Their words alone will not communicate to your audience what else is happening in their minds or on stage.
   - You may need to look at Shakespeare's *Romeo and Juliet* (Act I Scene v), to find out what happens and what people say.

Over to you!

Take another scene from *Romeo and Juliet*, for example, the famous balcony scene (Act II Scene ii) or the death of Tybalt (Act III Scene i), and re-write it as a modern playscript.

Decide on the two opposing families and the reason for their tension, for example:

- black and white (a racial drama)
- Catholic and Hindu (a religious drama)
- rich and poor (a social drama).

Think then about how this impacts upon the setting of the play.

- What will the characters say? How will they say it?
- What other characters will be present? What character could replace the 'nurse', whom we would not have today?
- What stage directions would you have to give for any fighting?
- Keep to the conventions of playscripts.

12 Genre: science fiction

The author, H.G. Wells, describes an alien emerging from its spacecraft.

I saw a young man, a shop assistant in Woking I believe he was, standing on the cylinder and trying to scramble out of the hole again. The crowd had pushed him in. The end of the cylinder was being screwed out from within. Nearly two feet of shining screw projected. Somebody blundered against me, and I narrowly missed being pitched onto the top of the screw. I turned, and as I did so the screw must have come out, for the lid of the cylinder fell upon the gravel with a ringing concussion. I stuck my elbow into the person behind me, and turned my head towards the thing again. For a moment that circular cavity seemed perfectly black. I had the sunset in my eyes.

I think everyone expected to see a man emerge – possibly something a little unlike us terrestrial men, but in all essentials a man. I know I did. But, looking, I presently saw something stirring within the shadow:

greyish billowy movements, one above another, and then two luminous disks – like eyes. Then something resembling a little grey snake, about the thickness of a walking stick, coiled up out of the writhing middle, and wriggled in the air towards me – and then another.

A sudden chill came over me. There was a loud shriek from a woman behind. I half turned, keeping my eyes fixed upon the cylinder still, from which other tentacles were now projecting, and began pushing my way back from the edge of the pit. I saw astonishment giving place to horror on the faces of the people about me. I heard inarticulate exclamations on all sides. There was a general movement backwards. I saw the shopman struggling still on the edge of the pit. I found myself alone, and saw the people on the other side of the pit running off, Stent among them. I looked again at the cylinder, and ungovernable terror gripped me. I stood petrified and staring.

A big greyish rounded bulk, the size, perhaps, of a bear, was rising slowly and painfully out of the cylinder. As it bulged up and caught the light, it glistened like wet leather. Two large dark-coloured eyes were regarding me steadfastly. The mass that framed them, the head of the thing, was rounded, and had, one might say, a face. There was a mouth under the eyes, the lipless brim of which quivered and panted, and dropped saliva. The whole creature heaved and pulsated convulsively. A lank tentacular appendage gripped the edge of the cylinder, another swayed in the air.

Those who have never seen a living Martian can scarcely imagine the strange horror of its appearance. The peculiar V-shaped mouth with its pointed upper lip, the absence of brow ridges, the absence of a chin beneath the wedgelike lower lip, the incessant quivering of this mouth, the

Gorgon groups of tentacles, the tumultuous breathing of the lungs in a strange atmosphere, the evident heaviness and painfulness of movement due to the greater gravitational energy of the earth – above all, the extraordinary intensity of the immense eyes – were at once vital, intense, inhuman, crippled and monstrous. There was something fungoid in the oily brown skin, something in the clumsy deliberation of the tedious movements unspeakably nasty. Even at this first encounter, this first glimpse, I was overcome with disgust and dread.

Suddenly the monster vanished. It had toppled over the brim of the cylinder and fallen into the pit, with a thud like the fall of a great mass of leather. I heard it give a peculiar thick cry, and forthwith another of these creatures appeared darkly in the deep shadow of the aperture. I turned and, running madly, made for the first group of trees, perhaps a hundred yards away; but I ran slantingly and stumbling, for I could not avert my face from these things. There, among some young pine trees and furze bushes, I stopped, panting, and waited further developments. The common round the sand pits was dotted with people, standing like myself in a half-fascinated terror, staring at these creatures, or rather at the heaped gravel at the edge of the pit in which they lay. And then, with a renewed horror, I saw a round, black object bobbing up and down on the edge of the pit. It was the head of the shopman who had fallen in, but showing as a little black object against the hot western sun. Now he got his shoulder and knee up, and again he seemed to slip back until only his head was visible. Suddenly he vanished, and I could have fancied a faint shriek had reached me. I had a momentary impulse to go back and help him that my fears overruled. Everything was then quite invisible, hidden by the deep pit and the heap of sand that the fall of the cylinder had made.

Anyone coming along the road from Chobham or Woking would have been amazed at the sight – a dwindling multitude of perhaps a hundred people or more standing in a great irregular circle, in ditches, behind bushes, behind gates and hedges, saying little to one another and that in short, excited shouts, and staring, staring hard at a few heaps of sand. The barrow of ginger beer stood, a queer derelict, black against the burning sky, and in the sand pits was a row of deserted vehicles with their horses feeding out of nosebags or pawing the ground.

from *War of the Worlds*
by H.G. Wells

Read on!

1. List three things you would expect to see in a book marked 'science fiction'.
2. Where have you gained your awareness of science fiction as a genre? From film? From books? From comics?
3. Why do you think so many people enjoy writing in this genre?
4. Show how the author involves all your senses in this description of the alien and its behaviour.

Seeing	Hearing	Feeling

5. Why might an appeal to your senses be more important in science fiction than in another genre? How else can you understand something beyond your usual understanding?
6. List adjectives from the passage which suggest the horror of this creature – unlike anything the author has seen on earth, for example, 'billowy movements', 'bulging eyes'.
7. List some comparisons used in the passage which enable you to imagine the alien, for example, 'resembling a little grey snake'.

Write on!

1. Show how Wells has planned the suspense of the episode by allowing the creature to emerge slowly, stage by stage. Copy and complete the chart.

Stage	What you see	What you feel
Stage 1		
Stage 2		

2. Look closely at the vivid description of the alien. Extract the relevant details.
3. Continue Wells' science fiction story but involve another alien creature. Use the techniques identified so far – the slow emergence of aliens, maximising the horror with vivid, accurate details.

- How will the story develop?
- How will it be resolved?

Over to you!

Write your own story in this genre, following the structure shown in the diagram. The Activity Sheet will help.

- Think carefully about the setting: this world or another?
- Think about the era: present or future?
- How will you start?
- What kinds of characters and language will you use?
- You may like to consider storylines of films you have seen.

- Will it end 'happily ever after'?
- Try to avoid cliché – not all aliens are 'evil'.

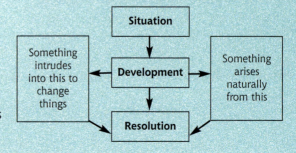

13 Genre: historical fiction

This passage is from a modern detective novel, but it is set in Ancient Rome.

The slave who came to fetch me on that unseasonably warm spring morning was a young man, hardly more than twenty.

Usually, when a client sends *for* me, the messenger is a slave from the very lowest rung of the household – a grub, a cripple, a half-wit boy from the stables stinking of dung and sneezing from the bits of straw in his hair. It's a kind of formality; when one seeks out the services of Gordianus the Finder, one keeps a certain distance and restraint. It's as if I were a leper, or the priest of some unclean Oriental cult. I'm used to it. I take no offence – so long as my accounts are paid on time and in full.

The slave who stood at my door on this particular morning, however, was very clean and meticulously groomed. He had a quiet manner that was respectful but far from grovelling – the politeness one expects from any young man addressing another man ten years his elder. His Latin was impeccable (better than mine), and the voice that delivered it was as beautifully modulated as a flute. No grub from the stables, then, but clearly the educated and pampered servant of a fond master. The slave's name was Tiro.

'Of the household of the most esteemed Marcus Tullius Cicero,' he added, pausing with a slight inclination of his head to see if I recognised the name. I did not. 'Come to seek your services,' he added, 'on the recommendation of …'

I took his arm, placed my forefinger over his lips, and led him into the house. Brutal winter had been followed by sweltering spring; despite the early hour, it was already far too hot to be standing in an open doorway. It was also far too early to be listening to this young slave's chatter, no matter how melodious his voice. My temples rolled with thunder. Spidery traces of lightning flashed and vanished just beyond the corners of my eyes.

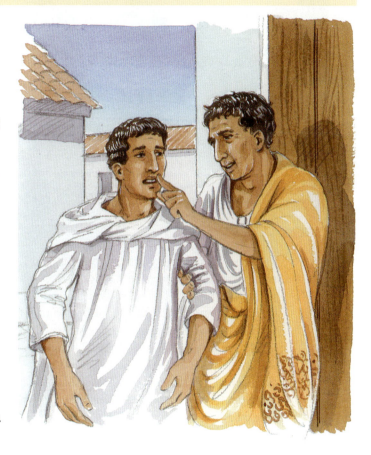

'Tell me,' I said, 'do you know the cure for a hangover?'

Young Tiro looked at me sidelong, puzzled by the change of subject, suspicious of my sudden familiarity. 'No, sir.'

I nodded. 'Perhaps you've never experienced a hangover?'

He blushed slightly. 'No, sir.'

'Your master allows you no wine?'

'Of course he does. But as my master says, moderation in all things …'

I nodded. I winced. The slightest movement set off an excruciating pain. 'Moderation in all things, I suppose, except the hour at which he sends a slave to call at my door.'

'Oh. Forgive me, sir. Perhaps I should return at a later hour?'

Genre: historical fiction

'That would be a waste of your time and mine. Not to mention your master's. No, you'll stay, but you'll speak no business until I tell you to, and you'll join me for breakfast in the garden, where the air is sweeter.'

I took his arm again, led him through the atrium, down a darkened hallway, and into the peristyle at the centre of the house. I watched his eyebrows rise in surprise, whether at the extent of the place or its condition I couldn't be sure. I was used to the garden, of course, but to a stranger it must have appeared quite a shambles – the willow trees madly overgrown, their hanging tendrils touching tall weeds that sprouted from dusty ground; the fountain at the centre long ago run dry, its little marble statue of Pan pocked with age; the narrow pond that meandered through the garden opaque and stagnant, clogged with Egyptian rushes growing out of control. The garden had gone wild long before I inherited the house from my father, and I had done nothing to repair it. I preferred it as it was – an uncontrolled

place of wild greenness hidden away in the midst of orderly Rome, a silent vote for chaos against mortared bricks and obedient shrubbery. Besides, I could never have afforded the labour and materials to have the garden put back into formal condition.

'I suppose this must be rather different from your master's house.' I sat in one chair, gingerly so as not to disturb my head, and indicated that Tiro should take the other. I clapped my hands and instantly regretted the noise. I bit back the pain and shouted, 'Bethesda! Where is that girl? She'll bring us food in a moment. That's why I answered the door myself – she's busy in the pantry. Bethesda!'

Tiro cleared his throat. 'Actually, sir, it's rather larger than my master's.'

I looked at him blankly, my stomach rumbling now in competition with my temples. 'What's that?'

'The house, sir. Bigger than my master's.'

'That surprises you?'

He looked down, fearing he had offended me.

'Do you know what I do for a living, young man?'

'Not exactly, sir.'

'But you know it's something not quite respectable – at least insofar as anything is worthy of respect in Rome these days. But not illegal – at least insofar as legality has any meaning in a city ruled by a dictator. So you're surprised to find me living in such spacious quarters, as ramshackle as they may be. That's perfectly all right. I'm sometimes surprised myself. And there you are, Bethesda. Set the tray here, between me and my unexpected but perfectly welcome young guest.'

from *Roman Blood*
by Steven Saylor

Glossary

atrium an inner courtyard open to the sky
peristyle an open space enclosed by columns

Read on!

1   This story is set in Ancient Rome. What does this add to the atmosphere?

2   What do you find strange about how the characters speak, considering this story is set in Ancient Rome? How would they have spoken in reality?

3   What do you find interesting about the way the characters act and react? Is this what you would have expected from this historical period? Give reasons.

4   What things can you recognise in the passage which are still with us today?

What things are 'historical'? Use this chart to help:

Item or concept	Roman only	Modern also
Slaves		
Hangover		

5   How does the first sentence of the novel firmly fix the story in the historical period?

6   List other details from the passage which show how the writer establishes the historical period, for instance details about his house and garden.

Write on!

Continue with the next episode of this Roman detective novel.

- Why has the slave come? Are there any clues in the narrative?
- What mystery does Gordianus solve?
- What conventions of the detective story will you use?
- Think about Roman details you will use for the story, for instance, there will be no phones or cars.
- Use specialist language from history – for example, the Roman central heating system (hypocaust) or an army leader (centurion) – to make the story more accurate and credible. Research and record the vocabulary you find. The Activity Sheet will help.

Over to you!

Choose another historical period in which to set a detective novel, for example the French Revolution, but this time use a female detective as the main character.

- Use the format of the passage, which opens when the detective is visited by a servant.
- Give a strong sense of the character of the detective from the start by what she says.
- Use relevant detail to create a sense of the era (the 'historical context') as well as how the characters think and feel about this.
- What problems might a woman face at this time, as a detective?
- Use the Activity Sheet to help you to collect appropriate detail: for example, how will your detective travel (no fast getaway cars)? How will your detective communicate over distance (no phones)?
- Use a simple plan: situation, development and resolution.
- Use any features of detective fiction you know.

14 Genre: the Western

Ledyard was a small, thin-featured man, a peddler or trader who came through every couple of months with things you could not get at the general store in town. He would pack his stock on a mule-team freighter driven by an old, white-haired Negro who acted like he was afraid even to speak without permission. Ledyard would make deliveries in his buckboard, claiming a hard bargain always and picking up orders for articles to bring on the next trip. I did not like him, and not just because he said nice things about me he did not mean for father's benefit. He smiled too much and there was no real friendliness in it.

By the time we were beside the porch, he had swung the horse into our lane and was pulling it to a stop. He jumped down, calling greetings. Father went to meet him. Shane stayed by the porch, leaning against the end post.

'It's here,' said Ledyard. 'The beauty I told you about.' He yanked away the canvas covering from the body of the wagon and the sun was bright on a shiny new seven-pronged cultivator lying on its side on the floorboards. 'That's the best buy I've toted this haul.'

'Hm-m-m-m,' said father. 'You've hit it right. That's what I've been wanting. But when you start chattering about a best buy that always means big money. What's the tariff?'

'Well, now.' Ledyard was slow with his reply. 'It cost me more than I figured when we was talking last time. You might think it a bit steep. I don't. Not for a new beauty like that there. You'll make up the difference in no time with the work you'll save with that. Handles so easy even the boy here will be using it before long.'

'Pin it down,' said father. 'I've asked you a question.'

Ledyard was quick now. 'Tell you what, I'll shave the price, take a loss to please a good customer. I'll let you have it for a hundred and ten.'

I was startled to hear Shane's voice cutting in quiet and even and plain. 'Let you have it? I reckon he will. There was one like that in a store in Cheyenne. List price sixty dollars.'

Ledyard shifted part way around. For the first time he looked closely at our visitor. The surface smile left his face. His voice held an ugly undertone. 'Did anyone ask you to push in on this?'

'No,' said Shane, quietly and evenly as before. 'I reckon no one did.' He was still leaning against the post. He did not move and he did not say anything more. Ledyard turned to father, speaking rapidly.

'Forget what he says, Starrett. I've spotted him now. Heard of him half a dozen times along the road up here. No one knows him. No one can figure him. I think I can. Just a stray wandering through, probably chased out of some town and hunting cover. I'm surprised you'd let him hang around.'

'You might be surprised at a lot of things,' said father, beginning to bite off his words. 'Now give it to me straight on the price.'

'It's what I said. A hundred and ten. Hell, I'll be out money on the deal anyway, so I'll shave it to a hundred if that'll make you feel any better.' Ledyard hesitated, watching father. 'Maybe he did see something in Cheyenne. But he's mixed up. Must have been one of those little makes – flimsy and barely half the size. That might match his price.'

Father did not say anything. He was looking at Ledyard in a steady, unwavering way. He had not even glanced at Shane. You might have believed he had not even heard what Shane had said. But his lips were folding in to a tight line like he was thinking what was not pleasant to think. Ledyard waited and father did not say anything and the climbing anger in Ledyard broke free.

'Starrett. Are you going to stand there and let that – that tramp nobody knows about call me a liar? Are you going to take his word over mine? Look at him! Look at his clothes! He's just a cheap, tinhorn –'

Ledyard stopped, choking on whatever it was he had meant to say. He fell back a step with a sudden fear showing in his face. I knew why even as I turned my head to see Shane. That same chill I had felt the day before, intangible and terrifying, was in the air again. Shane was no longer leaning against the porch post. He was standing erect, his hands clenched at his sides, his eyes boring at Ledyard, his whole body alert and alive in the leaping instant.

You felt without knowing how that each teetering second could bring a burst of indescribable deadliness. Then the tension passed, fading in the empty silence. Shane's eyes lost their sharp focus on Ledyard and it seemed to me that reflected in them was some pain deep within him.

Father had pivoted so that he could see the two of them in the one sweep. He swung back to Ledyard alone.

'Yes, Ledyard, I'm taking his word. He's my guest. He's here at my invitation. But that's not the reason – .' Father straightened a little and his head went up and he gazed into the distance beyond the river. 'I can figure men for myself. I'll take his word on anything he wants to say any day of God's whole year.'

Father's head came down and his voice was flat and final. 'Sixty is the price. Add ten for a fair profit, even though you probably got it wholesale. Another ten for hauling it here. That tallies to eighty. Take that or leave that. Whatever you do, snap to it and get off my land.'

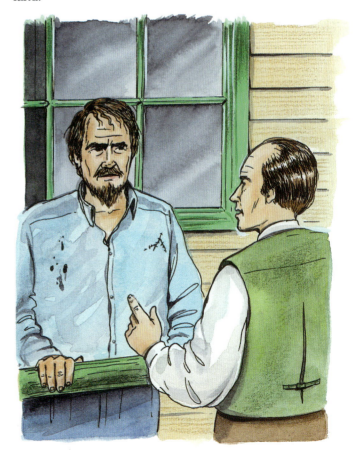

Genre: the Western

Ledyard stared down at his hands, rubbing them together as if they were cold. 'Where's your money?' he said.

Father went into the house, into the bedroom where he kept our money in a little leather bag on the closet shelf. He came back with the crumpled bills. All this while Shane stood there, not moving, his face hard, his eyes following father with a strange wildness in them that I could not understand.

Ledyard helped father heave the cultivator to the ground, then jumped to the wagon seat and drove off like he was glad to get away from our place. Father and I turned from watching him into the road. We looked around for Shane and he was not in sight. Father shook his head in wonderment. 'Now where do you suppose –' he was saying, when we saw Shane coming out of the barn.

He was carrying an axe, the one father used for heavy kindling. He went directly around the corner of the building. We stared after him and we were still staring when we heard it, the clear ringing sound of steel biting into wood.

I never could have explained what that sound did to me. It struck through me as no single sound had ever done before. With it ran a warmth that erased at once and forever the feelings of sudden chill terror that our visitor had evoked in me. There were sharp hidden hardnesses in him. But these were not for us. He was dangerous as mother had said. But not to us as father too had said. And he was no longer a stranger. He was a man like father in whom a boy could believe in – the simple knowing that what was beyond comprehension was still clean and solid and right.

from *Shane*
by Jack Schaefer

Read on!

1 List three things you would expect to find in a 'Western'. Where have you learned about this genre?
2 Does this passage contain any of the features you expected?
3 Show how the writer immediately lets the reader know the genre of the story.

Equipment	
Animals	
Place names	

4 How can you tell what Ledyard feels about Shane?
5 In comparison, explain how the boy feels about Shane. Give examples to show how his feelings change.
6 Why do you think the author uses so much speech in this extract? What does it add to the sense of 'the West'.
7 How do you know that Shane is 'a hero' in terms of the 'Western', even though he does very little in the extract?

Write on!

1 There is little physical description of Shane in the passage – more of a sense of his power – and yet he is the key figure. Summarise what we know about him.

What he says and how he says it	Characteristics	How others react to him

2 Write a description of Shane for a newspaper of the time, as if he were a 'Wanted' character.

3 Shane uses the axe to help Bob's father remove a tree stump which has previously been impossible to move. Continue the story. Consider such questions as:

- Why did Shane help to remove the old stump in the yard?
- How does this strengthen the relationship between the two men?
- What will happen afterwards?
- How does the boy, Bob, get involved in the story?
- How will the story resolve?

Over to you!

Take one particular theme of the Western genre – the mysterious brave hero.

- These people often appear from 'nowhere' and are loners.
- As such, people are suspicious of them.
- They act as a force for good and defeat the 'bad guys' at the end.
- They usually 'ride away into the sunset'.

Use this structure to write your own Western story. Research if necessary to collect accurate detail to make the narrative believable. The Activity Sheet will help.

- Ensure that your first paragraph establishes the era and the genre for your audience.

15 Personal stories

One day, when I was about ten, and leaning over a showcase as usual, I found a man at my side. He said, 'Excuse me, sonny.' He moved me away from the case and opened it with a key. I watched him with respect for he was a curator. He was one with my heroes, Schliemann, Pitt-Rivers, and Flinders-Petrie, men I believed in touch with levels and explanations that would have surprised them had they known. In some sense, this curator had the hot sand, the molten sun of Egypt lying in his turnups. I felt his tweedy jacket had been windblown on a dozen sites. He was big. Was he not what I wanted to become? His face was a little fat, and reddened. There was a ring of sandy curls round the baldness of his head. He was a cheerful man, as I soon discovered, whistling in the hush as if it were not sacred, but so habitual as to be unnoticed. He hummed sometimes to himself, as he arranged the amulets in a pattern which pleased him better. He took notice of me, questioned me, and soon found out that I was as learned an Egyptologist as I could well be, considering my age. At last he asked me – who desired nothing better – if I would like to give him a hand with some work he had to do. We went together through a museum I already felt to be more personally mine, I in the shorts, jersey, socks and shoes of an English schoolboy, he in his tweedy jacket and baggy flannels. We passed out of the Egyptian department, through the hall devoted to relics of the Industrial Revolution, through another hall full of stuffed animals, and up wide, marble stairs to the geology department. One corner of the room had been partitioned off from the rest. There was no ceiling to this part, as I discovered when the curator opened the door with another key and I followed him in. It was a makeshift division in what had once been a room of a splendid and princely house. But it was a division full of significance. There were rows of green filing cabinets, with papers sticking out of the drawers. There were shelves of books, proceedings of learned societies, and other expensive volumes that I had heard of but could not afford. Lying open on a desk was the British Museum facsimile of the *Book of the Dead* in all its rich colour. Wherever I looked things added up into an image of the life I guessed at but had not known, the world of the wise men, the archaeologists. There was a diorite vase, surely from the depths of the Step Pyramid; there was a Greek dish, from Alexandria, perhaps, but most scandalously misused, since I saw a fat roll of cigarette ash in it, and a curl of half-burnt paper. There were predynastic flint knives, and in one corner of the room a broken, sandstone altar, its scooped-out channels waiting patiently for blood.

But all these, which I took in at a glance, were nothing to the main exhibits. A sarcophagus, tilted like a packing case, leaned against the left-hand wall. The lid leaned against the wall alongside it, the inner surface revealing a white painting of Nut the Sky Goddess. I could see how the lid had been anthropomorphized, indicating by its curves the swelling of hips and chest, the neat hair, the feet. But the painted face was hidden in shadow, and stared away from us at the wall. Nor did I try long to see the face, because the lid and the box were no more than a preliminary. Before me, only a foot or two away on a trestle table, head back, arms crossed, lay a wrapped and bandaged mummy.

There was a new kind of atmosphere, some different quality in the space between me and it, because no glass kept me away. Glass multiplies space, and things in glass cases have an illogical quality of remoteness. I was not prepared for this difference; and I was not prepared for the curator's casual habitual approach. He stood on the other side of the mummy, hands resting on the table and looked at me cheerfully.

'You can give me a hand with this, if you like.'

I could have shaken my head, but I nodded, for my fate was on me. I guess that my eyes were big, and my mouth pinched a little. Yet at the same time there was an excitement in me that was either a part of or at war with – I am not certain which – my awe and natural distaste for the object. If I have to define my state of mind I should say it consisted in a rapid oscillation between unusual extremes; and this oscillation made me a little unsteady on my feet, a little unsure of the length of my legs; and like a ground bass to all this turmoil was the knowledge that by my approach, by my complicity, by the touch which must surely take place of my hand on the dead dry skin, I was storing up a terrible succession of endless dark nights for myself.

But he had commenced without waiting for more than a nod from me. He was untying the long bandages that harnessed in the first shroud. As they came free, he handed them to me and told me to roll them up and put them on the side table. He hefted the thing itself and it turned on the table like another piece of wood. It was much harder inside the bandages and shrouds than you might suppose, turning with a sort of dull knock. He took off the outer shroud, a large oblong of

Personal stories

linen, now dark brown, which we folded, the two of us, as you might hold a bedsheet – he, holding one end for a moment with his chin. I knew what we should look for next. Each limb, each digit, was wrapped separately, and the amulets to ensure eternal security and happiness were hidden among the bandages. Presently they appeared one by one as we took the bandages away, little shapes of blue faience. It seemed to me in my wider oscillation, my swifter transition from hot to cold, that they were still warm from the hands of the embalmer/priest who was the last to touch them three thousand years ago, and who was surely standing with us now, whenever now was. But our operations had their own inevitability; and at last I laid my compelled, my quivering and sacrilegious hand on the thing itself, experienced beyond all question, the bone, and its binding of thick, leathery skin.

The curator glanced at his wristwatch and whistled, but with astonishment, this time.

'I've kept you late, sonny. You'd better go straight away. Apologize to your parents for me. You can come back tomorrow if you like.'

I left him standing alone or partly alone, where I knew I should never dare to stand myself. The face of the sarcophagus was still hidden against the wall, but the curator was smiling at me out of his round, red face, under a fringe of curly hair. He waved one hand, and there was a hank of browning bandage in it, above a brightly lit and eternally uncheerful grin. I hurried away through the deserted museum with my contaminated hands to the dark streets and the long trek home. There I told my parents and my brother in excited detail about what had happened, was crossquestioned, and finally prepared for the terrors of bed.

Now it is important to realize that I remembered and still remember everything in vivid and luminous detail. It became the event of my life; and before I returned to the museum, I talked the thing over passionately with my parents and myself. I suffered the terrors of bed. I wrote an essay describing the episode when I went to school, and got extravagant praise for it. I brooded constantly about the lid of the sarcophagus with its hidden face. Yet it is important to realize that none of the episode happened at all. From the moment when I stood by the showcase, brooding and desperate, wishing, as singlemindedly as the hero of a fairy tale, till the time when I ran helter-skelter down the museum steps, I was somewhere; and I still do not know where that was. There was no curator with a red, smiling face. There was no mummy, and no sarcophagus. There was a partitioned corner of the geological room, but it contained rolls of maps, not bandages. I looked at the place in daylight and knew myself to be a liar, though think now that a liar is exactly what I was. It was the childish equivalent of the Lost Weekend, the indulgence behind which was my unchildish learning, and my overwhelming need to come to terms with the Egyptian thing. The whole selfsupplying episode is a brilliant part of the Egypt from my inside.

Hot Gates
by William Golding

Read on!

1 This is an account from an autobiography. How does the first sentence show that this is a 'personal story'?

2 What is the boy's passion? What specialist words and phrases tell you this and add a sense of the 'real' to the narrative? You may need a dictionary to complete this chart. The Activity Sheet will help.

3 How might the author's enthusiasm for this hobby explain his behaviour at the end of the passage?

4 What details (for instance, the unwrapping of the mummy) show that the boy really does know the subject?

5 Why does the revelation at the end of the passage come as a shock? When you look back, what clues can suggest that this is going to happen?

6 Why did Golding think it was an important episode?

Write on!

1 Write what Golding said to his parents and his brother about the events.

- Use the details from the text.
- How was he cross-questioned?
- How would they react to his story?
- What would they think?
- How would he use his extensive and detailed knowledge to convince them?

2 Write what Golding would have written at school about how he unwrapped the mummy.

- Use the detail from the passage.
- Use the correct terminology – he knew this well, since it was his hobby.
- Why were the procedures necessary?
- Explain how the boy felt about it.

Over to you!

Write an account of a deception you used as a child, to be included in your autobiography. Choose an event from your childhood (real or imaginary) to reflect one of your great interests. For example, were you 'discovered' singing by a pop promoter and offered a part in a West End show which you had to turn down? Were you allowed to strip the engine of a car by the manager of a garage?

- Follow the same plan as the passage.
- Explain at the end why you deceived people, but how it was an essential part of growing up.
- Follow the conventions of an autobiography (for instance, first person narration), use the past tense, include vital detail – this is why it is such a memory.

16 Memoirs

Richard Feynman (1918–88), the author of this passage, was jointly awarded the Nobel Prize for Physics in 1965 for his work on quantum electrodynamics.

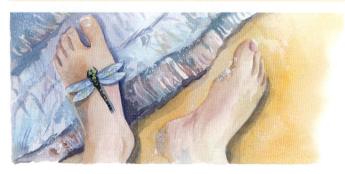

I had an insect book when I was about thirteen. It said that dragonflies are not harmful; they don't sting. In our neighborhood it was well known that 'darning needles', as we called them, were very dangerous when they'd sting. So if we were outside somewhere playing baseball, or something, and one of these things would fly around, everybody would run for cover, waving their arms, yelling, 'A darning needle! A darning needle!'

So one day I was sitting on the beach, and I'd just read this book that said dragonflies don't sting. A darning needle came along, and everybody was screaming and running around, and I just sat there. 'Don't worry!' I said, 'Darning needles don't sting!'

The thing landed on my foot. Everybody was yelling and it was a big mess, because this darning needle was sitting on my foot. And there I was, this scientific wonder, saying it wasn't going to sting me.

You're sure this is a story that's going to come out that it stings me – but it didn't. The book was right. But I did sweat a bit.

I also had a little hand microscope. It was a toy microscope, and I pulled the magnification piece out of it, and would hold it in my hand like a magnifying glass, even though it was a microscope of forty or fifty power. With care you could hold the focus. So I could go around and look at things right out in the street.

When I was in graduate school at Princeton, I once took it out of my pocket to look at some ants that were crawling around on some ivy. I had to exclaim out loud, I was so excited. What I saw was an ant and an aphid, which ants take care of – they carry them from plant to plant if the plant they're on is dying. In return the ants get partially digested aphid juice, called 'honeydew'. I knew that; my father had told me about it, but I had never seen it.

So here was this aphid and sure enough, an ant came along, and patted it with its feet – all around the aphid, pat, pat, pat, pat, pat. This was terribly exciting! Then the juice came out of the back of the aphid. And because it was magnified, it looked like a big, beautiful, glistening ball, like a balloon, because of the surface tension. Because the microscope wasn't very good, the drop was colored a little bit from the chromatic aberration in the lens – it was a gorgeous thing!

The ant took this little ball in its two front feet, lifted it off the aphid, and held it. The world is so different at that scale that you can pick up water and hold it! The ants probably have a fatty or greasy material on their legs that doesn't break the surface tension of the water when they hold it up. Then the ant broke the surface of the drop with its mouth, and the surface tension collapsed the drop right into his gut. It was very interesting to see the whole thing happen!

from *Surely You're Joking, Mr. Feynman*
by Richard P. Feynman

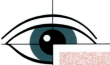

Read on!

Memoirs are different from autobiographies; they are not written in strict chronological order – they are selected episodes from the person's life.

1 In what ways is the subject matter of the memoirs of Richard Feynman similar to that of an autobiography?

2 For what audience are memoirs written? For what purpose? Compare these with the audience and purpose of an autobiography and a diary.

3 What do the episodes tell you about Richard Feynman's attitude to learning from books and from observations?

4 What feelings did Richard Feynman experience during his observations of ants and aphids? Which words and phrases express these feelings?

5 Look up 'honeydew'. Compare the definition with Feynman's description:

	Dictionary definition	Feynman's description
Details included		
How it helps you to picture what honeydew is like		
The style of language used (how formal and how personal)		
How the style of language affects your response		
The writer's relationship with the subject matter		
What you can tell from the text about the writer		

6 What can you tell about Feynman's personality? Explain your answer and support it by quoting from the passage.

Write on!

1 Analyse the characteristics of the style of language Feynman uses to describe his observations:

Characteristics of language	Effects
Punctuation	
Italics	
Personal pronouns	
Sentence lengths	
Verbs	
Adjectives	
Exclamations	

2 Re-write for a scientific textbook Richard Feynman's description of an ant collecting honeydew from an aphid. The Activity Sheet will help.

Consider:

• which observations and comments to keep and which to delete
• the changes which need to be made to the language.

Compare the altered version with the original and describe the effects of the changes.

Over to you!

Re-read a report you have written about an interesting investigation or observation made during a science lesson.

Re-write your report in a way which conveys excitement about your discovery. Use Richard Feynman's style as a model.

17   A recount

In the morning I walked to Porthmadog Station – not the Blaenau Ffestiniog let's-play-trains one, but the real British Rail one. The station was closed, but there were several people on the platform, all studiously avoiding each other's gaze and standing, I do believe, on the same spot on which they stood every morning. I am pretty certain of this because as I was standing there minding my own business, a man in a suit arrived and looked at first surprised and then cross to find me occupying what was evidently his square metre of platform. He took a position a few feet away and regarded me with an expression not a million miles from hate. How easy it is sometimes, I thought, to make enemies in Britain. All you have to do is

stand in the wrong spot or turn your car round in their driveway – this guy had NO TURNING written all over him – or inadvertently take their seat on a train, and they will quietly hate you to the grave.

Eventually a two-carriage Sprinter train came in and we all shuffled aboard. They really are the most comfortless, utilitarian, deeply unlovely trains, with their hard-edged seats, their mystifyingly simultaneous hot and cold draughts, their harsh lighting and, above all, their noxious colour scheme with all those orange stripes and hopelessly jaunty chevrons. Why would anyone think that train passengers would like to be surrounded by a lot of orange, particularly first thing in the morning? I longed for one of those old-style trains that you found when I first came to Britain, the ones that had no corridors but consisted of just a series of self-contained compartments, each a little world unto itself. There was always a frisson of excitement as you opened the carriage door because you never knew what you would find on the other side. There was something pleasingly intimate and random about sitting in such close proximity with total strangers. I remember once I was in one of these trains when one of the other passengers, a shy-looking young man in a trench coat, was abruptly and lavishly sick on the floor – it was during a flu epidemic – and then had the gall to stumble from the train at the next station, leaving three of us to ride on into the evening in silence, with pinched faces and tucked-in toes and behaving, in that most extraordinary British way, as if nothing had happened.

We followed a coastal route past broad estuaries and craggy hills beside the grey, flat expanse of Cardigan Bay. The towns along the way all had names that sounded like a cat bringing up a hairball: Llywyngwril, Morfa Mawddach, Llandecwyn, Dyffryn Ardudwy. At Penrhyndeudraeth the train filled with children of all ages, all in school uniforms. I

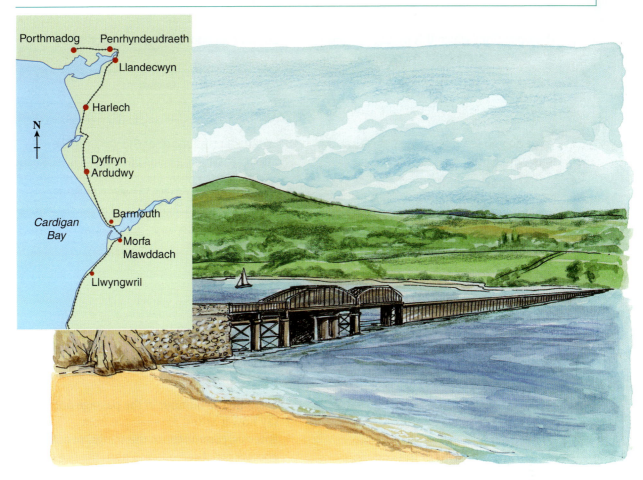

expected shouting and smoking and things to be flying about, but they were all impeccably behaved, every last one of them. They all departed at Harlech and the interior suddenly felt empty and quiet – quiet enough that I could hear the couple behind me conversing in Welsh, which pleased me. At Barmouth we crossed another broad estuary, on a rickety-looking wooden causeway. I had read somewhere that this causeway had been closed for some years and that Barmouth had until recently been the end of the line. It seemed a kind of miracle that BR had invested the money to repair the causeway and keep the line open, but I bet that if I were to come back in ten years, this trundling, half-forgotten line to Porthmadog will be in the hands of enthusiasts like those of the Blaenau Ffestiniog Railway and that some twit with a fussy little moustache will be telling me that I can't make the connection at Shrewsbury because it doesn't suit the society's timetable.

from *Notes From a Small Island*
by Bill Bryson

Glossary

BR British Rail, the organisation which used to run both the railways and the train services in Britain

Read on!

1 The book from which this passage comes describes a journey around Britain by rail, as shown on the map on page 54. In what ways is it more than a mere recount?

2 How can you tell, from the text, that the writer is not British?

3 What do you learn from the passage about the writer's opinions of:

   a) the British people?
   b) railways and trains in Britain?

Support all your answers by quoting from the text.

Opinions	Quotations

4 What assumptions does the writer make about particular groups of people?

Assumption	Evidence to support or refute it, or 'none'

Write on!

1 The passage includes some very precise observations of people's behaviour, which are interpreted by the writer as the sense of 'territory' which some people have (as on the railway platform in the opening paragraph).

   a) List any examples of this common type of behaviour which you or others in your group have come across, saying where it happened and what 'territory' the people were guarding.

   b) Describe what the people did in order to make others feel unwelcome in their 'territory'.

2 Examine the humour in the passage and say how it arises, for example from amusing comments on the things, people and events observed, and from the use of words.

3 What type of humour is it? (For example, slapstick, satire, situational.)

Over to you!

Make notes during any journeys you make, however short. Include details of:

* where your journey began, the time of day, what you did and your destination
* observations of the things you passed and any thoughts you had about them
* observations of the people you encountered: what they did, their facial expressions, body language and what they said (and how), and what might lie behind these actions, expressions and words.

Use Bill Bryson's style as a model: pick out the observations which interest you because of what they bring to mind, especially if they amuse you in any way; include details of people's actions and looks, and what lies behind them.

18   Information from books

Roman Games and Gladiators

Like the Greek theatre, the Roman Games (*ludi*) had a religious context. The oldest and grandest were the *Ludi Magni*, which in early times were vowed in honour of Jupiter *Optimus Maximus* by successful generals celebrating a victory. Gradually, it seems, these games became an annual event, and by 366 BC they were held every September. Later still, more games were instituted on an annual basis and they became a permanent and frequent element in the Roman religious calendar. By the late Republic the games were organised and paid for by serving magistrates who sought to further their own careers by pleasing the electorate through the entertainment they provided. The original idea of the games as a celebration in honour of the gods was eclipsed by their increasing role as an advertisement promoting the ambitions of men. *Panem et circenses* (bread and circuses), as Juvenal put it, were what the people came to expect as of right, and men in public office had to dig deep into their own pockets to oblige them.

The games consisted traditionally of a grand procession followed by chariot racing, staged animal hunts and drama. Gladiatorial combat was not at first part of the games, having, as we shall see, a different origin. Theatrical productions ranged from Roman adaptations of Greek forms of drama to more popular types of farce. By the second century BC, there were on the one hand the Greek-style comedies of Terence and Plautus and on the other the so-called mimes, a particularly popular and peculiarly Roman blend of satire and buffoonery, performed without the usual mask. The Roman authorities were fully aware not only of the political expediency of these entertainments,

Information from books

but also of their potential as 'opium of the people'. The emperor Augustus is reported to have censured a popular actor in the mimes called Pylades, whose petty quarrels and jealousies had become the talk of Rome. With calculated coolness he replied: 'It is to your advantage, Caesar, that the people should keep their thoughts on us.'

Chariot racing in Rome was staged in the Circus Maximus, situated in a valley between the Palatine and Aventine hills. Races had been held here since the days when Rome was ruled by kings. In time the racetrack was enlarged and equipped with seats for the spectators. The crowd, it seems, was composed of both men and women, sitting together – at the theatre and the amphitheatre the sexes were separated. The Circus underwent successive modifications and improvements. In 46 BC, for example, Julius Caesar enlarged it to the east and west and surrounded it with a moat filled with water, presumably to make the area safe for spectators watching wild beast shows.

Earlier, in 55 BC, iron barriers separating the crowd from the sports ground had given way at the games sponsored by Pompey in which armed Spanish Gaetuhans were set to fight twenty elephants. Under the Empire such bloody spectacles were usually reserved for the amphitheatre.

The chariot races themselves became highly organised affairs. Independently owned stables were established to cater for the demand for trained racehorses, and these were hired out, together with their drivers, to the magistrates funding the games. Passionate rivalry grew up between the stables. They developed their own followings, which were known as 'factions', identified by their colours: the Reds, Whites, Blues and Greens … The charioteers themselves were mostly slaves, many of whom must have been born to the stables from fathers who had followed the same profession. Successful charioteers, like gladiators, became the darlings of the people and might make enough profit to buy their freedom.

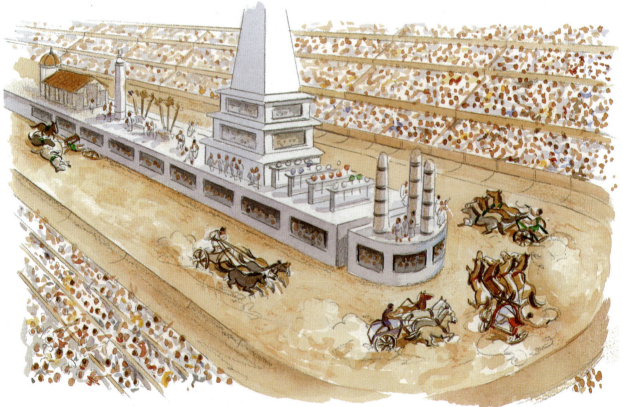

The Amphitheatre

The bloodier spectacles (*munera*) were also religious in origin. They were first held at funerals as a blood-offering to the deceased. Gladiators were sometimes known as *bustuarii*, or 'funeral men', and throughout their history the Romans continued to honour the memory of great men with gladiatorial contests. In the course of time, however, like the *ludi*, the *munera* became secularised as men in public life sought to secure the favour of the mob by pandering to its morbid tastes. Under the Empire it was the emperor's privilege to exploit the propaganda potential of *munera* by giving the most frequent, as well as the grandest, shows while at the same time limiting the number and size of those that could be given by others.

Rome did not acquire a stone-built arena until fairly late. At first *munera* were held in the Circus or in the Forum. The first permanent amphitheatre was built in 29 BC but was destroyed in the great fire of AD 64. It was replaced by the Colosseum, begun under Vespasian but not dedicated until AD 80 in the reign of the emperor Titus. Today the building, with its imposing arches arranged in three tiers, stands as one of the most remarkable products of Roman engineering. It is calculated to have had seating capacity for 45,000 people and standing room for a further 5,000. Underground there were cages for the wild beasts and a water system capable of flooding the arena for mock sea-battles.

The organisation of *munera* left nothing to chance. In the Italian townships and the provinces of the Empire the local magistrates who funded the shows as part of their civic duty contracted the job of mounting the events to a middleman (*lanista*). The latter maintained a stable of gladiators, trained at

Information from books

The fight was to the death. When a victim fell dead or was fatally wounded he was approached by an official disguised as Charon, the ferryman of the Underworld who carried a wooden mallet, and struck the unfortunate individual on the head. If the loser fell exhausted or only slightly wounded, then an appeal could be made to the emperor for mercy. The emperor would usually make his decision on the basis of what the crowd wished. His verdict was signalled with either an extended or a down-turned thumb.

Gladiatorial combat, although gruesome enough, was by no means the most brutal aspect of the *munera*. We hear, for example, of pairs of condemned criminals being driven into the arena, one armed and the other dressed only in a tunic. When, inevitably, the first had killed the second, the 'victor' was disarmed to become the victim of a new opponent, who was armed as he had been. Animals, too, provided the means for various forms of butchery. Wild beasts, enraged to distraction, were matched against each other in a fight to the death. Mock hunts were set up, in which huge numbers of exotic beasts were cruelly slaughtered by so-called *bestiarii*. During the *munera* held by Titus to celebrate the inauguration of the Colosseum, no fewer than 5,000 wild beasts were slaughtered in a single day.

We may justifiably feel revolted by such wanton acts of cruelty and express bewilderment at the Roman desire to gape at it. All the more disturbing is the fact that, although there were some dissenting voices among Stoic philosophers and, later, Christian moralists, the amphitheatre appears to have been attended by men and women from all levels of society. It was not only the common rabble who found pleasure in such spectacles; they were also attended and apparently enjoyed by men of taste and letters.

from *Greek and Roman Life*
by Ian Jenkins

their own expense, and would hire them out. At Rome it was the duty of magistrates known as *procuratores* to organise the *munera* in the name of the emperor, whose gladiators were recruited from a regular supply of prisoners of war and condemned criminals. At a show attended by the emperor it was the dubious privilege of the contestants to address him before the fighting began with the greeting: '*Ave Imperator, morituri te salutant*' (Hail Emperor, those who are about to die salute you).

The proceedings began with a grand parade, the gladiators dressed in gold and purple robes riding in chariots to the arena. Music was from a variety of brass and wind instruments and a hydraulic organ. The combatants were paired by lot and armed according to their respective categories: for example, a *retiarius* carried a net and a trident while a *samnite* carried a large oblong shield (*scutum*), a sword (*gladius*) or a spear (*hasta*) and was protected by a visored helmet, a greave on the right leg and a protective sleeve on the right arm.

Read on!

1 Write three things which come to mind when you think of 'Roman games and gladiators'. Where have you learned them?

2 How does reading the information change your perception of what it might have been like to live in Ancient Rome?

3 From which kind of book do you think this passage was taken? Why?

4 Who would be the audience for such a book?

5 Why does the author make use of so many Latin words and phrases?

6 List facts which you find surprising or shocking. Say why.

Facts which are surprising or shocking	Why
The Games started as a religious event	

Write on!

1 The writer's use of technical terms and Latin words show that he has researched his subject. List these words and make a glossary to help other readers to understand the passage more easily.

2 One way of extracting information in order to make use of it in other ways is to ask yourself key questions. Find information which answers questions about Roman games and gladiators. The Activity Sheet will help.

3 Follow the same procedure to extract information about the amphitheatre and what took place in it.

Over to you!

Having extracted the relevant and important information, you can use it in different ways in your writing.

1 Using the information, write an account of the Roman games for young children. Your audience is different and there will be restrictions on content (too bloodthirsty) and on language (too difficult).

2 Use information from the passage to write a promotional leaflet for chariot racing in Rome.

- Answer key questions about the races to provide accurate detail.
- Note examples and terminology which can be used to make the leaflet sound authentic.
- Decide for which audience the leaflet is intended.
- Think about stylistic features.

19 Information from electronic texts

Earthquakes

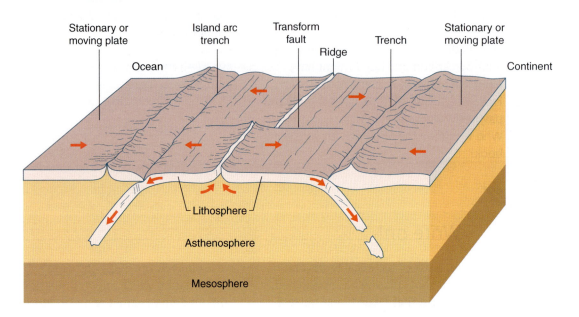

A three-dimensional diagram showing the movement of plates on the Earth's surface

Geographic concentrations of earthquakes

The Earth's major earthquakes occur mainly in belts coinciding with the margins of tectonic plates (*see above*).

One major earthquake belt passes around the Pacific Ocean and affects coastlines bordering on it, as, for example, those of New Zealand, New Guinea, Japan, the Aleutian Islands, Alaska and the western regions of North and South America. About 80 per cent of the energy presently released in earthquakes comes from those whose epicentres are in this belt. The seismic activity is not uniform throughout the belt, and there is a number of branches at various points.

A second belt passes through the Mediterranean region eastward through Asia and joins the first belt in the East Indies. The energy released in earthquakes from this belt is about 15 per cent of the world total. There are also striking connected belts of seismic activity, mainly along mid-oceanic ridges –

including those in the Arctic Ocean, the Atlantic Ocean, and the western Indian Ocean – and along the rift valleys of East Africa.

Most other parts of the world experience at least occasional shallow earthquakes – those which originate within 60 kilometres of the Earth's outer surface. The great majority of earthquakes are shallow.

Tectonic associations

There is a clear correspondence between the geographical distribution of volcanoes and major earthquakes, particularly in the circum-Pacific earthquake belts and along mid-oceanic ridges. Volcanic vents, however, are generally at a distance of some hundreds of kilometres from the majority of the epicentres of major shallow earthquakes, and many earthquake sources occur nowhere near active volcanoes. Earthquakes of intermediate focal depth frequently occur directly below structures marked by volcanic vents, but there is probably no immediate causal connection between these earthquakes and the volcanic activity; both most likely result from the same tectonic processes.

Plate tectonics

This theory deals with the dynamics of the Earth's outer shell, the lithosphere. According to the theory, the lithosphere consists of about a dozen large plates and several small ones. These plates move relative to one another and interact at their boundaries, where they diverge, converge, or slip relatively harmlessly past one another. Such interactions are thought to be responsible for most of the seismic and volcanic activity of the Earth, although earthquakes and volcanoes are not wholly absent in plate interiors. While moving about, the plates cause mountains to rise where they push together and continents to fracture and oceans to form where they pull apart. The continents, sitting passively on the backs of plates, drift with them and thereby bring about continual changes in the Earth's geography.

from *Encyclopaedia Britannica* website:
www.britannica.co.uk

Read on!

1   List any words in the text which you need to look up. Look them up and note their meanings.
2   Make a glossary of all the words you looked up. You could use a two-column table on a word-processor to sort the words alphabetically.
3   What does the passage say about places in which earthquakes occur? Copy and complete the table in note form:

The majority of powerful earthquakes	
Other powerful earthquakes	
Less powerful earthquakes	

4   What questions could be answered by reading the passage? Write a quiz (with answers), consisting of ten questions, about the locations and causes of earthquakes.

Exchange quizzes with a partner and answer one another's questions.

Write on!

1   Evaluate the text. How well does it:

- inform you about the places in which earthquakes occur?
- explain why they happen there?
- explain what causes earthquakes?

Support your answers with examples from the text.

2   What questions does the passage raise?

a)   Say how you could use the electronic version of the text to find the answers.
b)   Use the electronic version of this or another electronic text to find the answers.

Look for 'hot spots' and links to other electronic texts, including those on the Internet.

Over to you!

Copy the text directly from www.britannica.co.uk, scan it or key it in. Simplify it and explain the locations and causes of earthquakes for a radio documentary for the general public.

The text for the documentary needs to engage and keep the interest of the audience.

a)   Keep track of the changes you make, using: 'Tools', 'Track changes', and so on.
b)   Exchange copies with a partner who adds any other changes which might help (you could do this using email).

c)   Read your marked-up text and use 'Tools', 'Track changes' and 'Accept or reject changes' to complete the editing.

Consider:

- *deleting parts of the text*
- *adding to the text*
- *using simpler language (simpler sentences and fewer 'difficult' words, although some specialist vocabulary can be kept, as long as it is explained)*
- *making the language more exciting.*

20 Using time

Embroidery

The dark porch air in the late afternoon was full of needle flashes, like a movement of gathered silver insects in the light. The three women's mouths twitched over their work. Their bodies lay back and then imperceptibly forward, so that the rocking chairs tilted and murmured. Each woman looked to her own hands, as if quite suddenly she had found her heart beating there.

'What time is it?'

'Ten minutes to five.'

'Got to get up in a minute and shell those peas for dinner.'

'But – ' said one of them.

'Oh yes, I forgot. How foolish of me …' The first woman paused, put down her embroidery and needle, and looked through the open porch door, through the warm interior of the quiet house, to the silent kitchen. There upon the table, seeming more like symbols of domesticity than anything she had ever seen in her life, lay the mound of fresh-washed peas in their neat, resilient jackets, waiting for her fingers to bring them into the world.

'Go hull them if it'll make you feel good,' said the second woman.

'No,' said the first. 'I won't. I just won't.'

The third woman sighed. She embroidered a rose, a leaf, a daisy on a green field. The embroidery needle rose and vanished.

The second woman was working on the finest, most delicate piece of embroidery of them all, deftly poking, finding, and returning the quick needle upon innumerable journeys. Her quick black glance was on each motion. A flower, a man, a road, a sun, a house; the scene grew under her hand, a miniature beauty, perfect in every threaded detail.

'It seems at times like this that it's always your hands you turn to,' she said, and the others nodded enough to make the rockers rock again.

'I believe,' said the first lady, 'that our souls are in our hands. For we do everything to the world with our hands. Sometimes I think we don't use our hands half enough; it's certain we don't use our heads.'

They all peered more intently at what their hands were doing. 'Yes,' said the third lady, 'when you look back on a whole lifetime, it seems you don't remember faces so much as hands and what they did.'

They recounted to themselves the lids they had lifted, the doors they had opened and shut, the flowers they had picked, the dinners they had made, all with slow or quick fingers, as was their manner or custom. Looking back, you saw a flurry of hands, like a magician's dream, doors popping wide, taps turned, brooms wielded, children spanked. The flutter of pink hands

Using time

was the only sound; the rest was a dream without voices.

'No supper to fix tonight or tomorrow night or the next night after that,' said the third lady.

'No windows to open or shut.'

'No coal to shovel in the basement furnace next winter.'

'No papers to clip cooking articles out of.'

And suddenly they were crying. The tears roiled softly down their faces and fell into the material upon which their fingers twitched.

'This won't help things,' said the first lady at last, putting the back of her thumb to each under-eyelid. She looked at her thumb and it was wet.

'Now look what I've done!' cried the second lady, exasperated. The others stopped and peered over. The second lady held out her embroidery. There was the scene, perfect except that while the embroidered yellow sun shone down upon the embroidered green field, and the embroidered brown road curved toward an embroidered pink house, the man standing on the road had something wrong with his face.

'I'll just have to rip out the whole pattern, practically, to fix it right,' said the second lady.

'What a shame!' They all stared intently at the beautiful scene with the flaw in it.

The second lady began to pick away at the thread with her little deft scissors flashing. The pattern came out thread by thread. She pulled and yanked, almost viciously. The man's face was gone. She continued to seize at the threads.

'What are you doing?' asked the other women.

They leaned and saw what she had done.

The man was gone from the road. She had taken him out entirely.

They said nothing, but returned to their own tasks.

'What time is it?' asked someone.

'Five minutes to five.'

'Is it supposed to happen at five o'clock?'

'Yes.'

'And they're not sure what it'll do to anything, really when it happens?'

'No, not sure.'

'Why didn't we stop them before it got this far and this big?'

'It's twice as big as ever before. No, ten times, maybe a thousand.'

'This isn't like the first one or a dozen later ones. This is different. Nobody knows what it might do when it comes.'

They waited on the porch in the smell of roses and cut grass. 'What time is it now?'

'One minute to five.'

The needles flashed silver fire. They swam like a tiny school of metal fish in the darkening summer air.

Far away a mosquito sound. Then something like a tremor of drums. The three women cocked their heads, listening.

'We won't hear anything, will we?'

'They say not.'

'Perhaps we're foolish. Perhaps we'll go right on, after five o'clock, shelling peas, opening doors, stirring soups, washing dishes, making lunches, peeling oranges ...'

'My, how we'll laugh to think we were frightened by an old experiment!' They smiled a moment at each other.

'It's five o'clock.'

At these words, hushed, they all busied themselves. Their fingers darted. Their faces were turned down to the motions they made. They made frantic patterns. They made lilacs and grass and trees and houses and rivers in the embroidered cloth. They said nothing, but you could hear their breath in the silent porch air.

Thirty seconds passed.

The second woman sighed finally and began to relax.

'I think I just *will* go shell those peas for supper,' she said. 'I …'

But she hadn't time even to lift her head. Somewhere, at the side of her vision, she saw the world brighten and catch fire. She kept her head down, for she knew what it was. She didn't look up, nor did the others, and in the last instant their fingers were flying; they didn't glance about to see what was happening to the country, the town, this house, or even this porch. They were only staring down at the design in their flickering hands.

The second woman watched an embroidered flower go. She tried to embroider it back in, but it went, and then the road vanished, and the blades of grass.

She watched a fire, in slow motion almost, catch upon the embroidered house and unshingle it, and pull each threaded leaf from the small green tree in the hoop, and she saw the sun itself pulled apart in the design. Then the fire caught upon the moving point of the needle while still it flashed; she watched the fire come along her fingers and arms and body, untwisting the yarn of her being so painstakingly that she could see it in all its devilish beauty, yanking out the pattern from the material at hand. What it was doing to the other women or the furniture or the elm tree in the yard, she never knew. For now, yes now! It was plucking at the white embroidery of her flesh, fine pink thread of her cheeks, and at last it found her heart, a soft red rose sewn with fire, and it burned the fresh, embroidered petals away, one by delicate one …

from *The Golden Apples of the Sun*
by Ray Bradbury

Read on!

1 From the title, what would you expect this short story to be about?
2 What actually happens at the end of the story? What detail tells you this, although nothing is directly stated?
3 What message is Ray Bradbury trying to communicate to his audience in this story?
4 Time is an important factor in the story – both in its style and in its content. How much real time does the story span?

5 Explain how the writer uses references to time to slow down the story – it is almost as if the story takes as long to read as the length of time it describes.
6 Why is time so important to the women in the story?
7 Why are the pictures in the embroidery so important in the story? How do they help you to understand the end?

Write on!

Write an extract from this story which would take place ten minutes earlier. Begin:

'What time is it?'

'Twenty minutes to five.'

• Use references to time to break the narrative and to show how slowly time appears to be passing for the women. The Activity Sheet provides an alternative planning approach.

• Try to create suspense for the reader. As you slow the story the reader is prevented from solving the mystery about why the women are so concerned with the time.
• Create characters for the women.
• Allow them to discuss what will happen and who or what is responsible.
• Use the pictures they are embroidering in a similar way – they are creating a world which will soon be destroyed.

Over to you!

Write about a group of people waiting for a disaster or important event. Use time to stress key moments, slow the time scale and create suspense and tension.

• Structure your story using chronological order.
• Make notes about the setting of your story, the era in which it will be set and how this may influence the characters (how they speak, act, and what they say).
• You could use a word-processing package to cut and paste, to experiment with different opening paragraphs. This helps you to find the most effective opening. For example, you might use 'flashback'.
• Consider the effects of restructuring your story. Do you want to use the traditional structure, as below, or some variety of it?

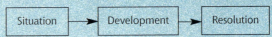

| Situation | → | Development | → | Resolution |

• One of the interesting aspects of this narrative is that you know how it will be resolved. The interest will come from the development of tension and from people's reactions.

21 A letter

This is from a translation of one of the many letters which Vincent van Gogh sent to his younger brother Theo.

[Arles, January 23, 1889]

My dear Theo,

Thank you for your letter and the 50 franc note it contained. I am now safe until the arrival of your next letter after the 1st. What happened about that money was entirely pure chance and misunderstanding, for which neither you nor I are responsible. By just the same mischance I could not telegraph as you said, because I did not know if you were still in Amsterdam or back in Paris. It is over now with the rest, and is one more proof of the proverb that misfortunes never come singly. Roulin left yesterday (of course my wire yesterday was sent off before the arrival of your letter of this morning). It was touching to see him with his children this last day, especially with the quite tiny one, when he made her laugh and jump on his knee, and sang for her.

I have just finished a new canvas which almost has what one might call a certain chic about it, a wicker basket with lemons and oranges, a cypress branch and a pair of blue gloves. You have already seen some of these baskets of fruit of mine.

Look here - you do know that what I am trying to do is to get back the money that my training as a painter has cost, neither more nor less. I have a right to that, and to the earning of my daily bread. I think it just that there should be that return, I don't say into your hands, since what we have done we have done together, and to talk of money distresses us so much. But let it go to your wife's hands, who will join with us besides in working with the artists.

If I am not yet devoting much thought to direct sales, it is because my count of pictures is not yet complete, but it is getting on, and I have set to work again with a nerve like iron.

A letter

I have good and ill luck in my production, but not ill luck only. For instance, if our Monticelli bunch of flowers is worth 500 francs to a collector, and it is, then I dare swear to you that my sunflowers are worth 500 francs too, to one of these Scots or Americans.

Now to get up heat enough to melt that gold, those flower-tones, it isn't any old person who can do it, it needs the force and concentration of a single individual whole and entire.

When I saw my canvases again after my illness the one which seemed the best to me was 'The Bedroom'.

The amount we handle is a respectable enough sum, I admit, but much of it runs away, and what we'll have to watch above all is that from year's end to year's end it doesn't all slip through the net. That is why as the month goes on I keep more or less trying to balance the outlay with the output, at least in relative terms. So many difficulties certainly do make me rather worried and timorous, but I haven't given up hope yet.

I have in hand the portrait of Roulin's wife, which I was working on before I was ill. In it I had ranged the reds from rose to an orange, which rose through the yellows to lemon, with light and sombre greens. If I could finish it, I should be very glad, but I am afraid she will no longer want to pose with her husband away.

You can see what a disaster Gauguin's leaving is, because it has thrust us down just when we had made a home and furnished it to take in our friends in bad times. Only in spite of it we will keep the furniture, etc. And though everyone will now be afraid of me, in time that may disappear.

We are all mortal and subject to all the ailments there are, and if the latter aren't exactly of an agreeable kind, what can one do about it? The best thing is to try and get rid of them.

I feel remorse too when I think of the trouble which, however involuntarily, I on my side caused Gauguin.

Meantime, the great thing is that your marriage should not be delayed … From me, your brother, you will not want completely banal congratulations and assurances that you are about to be transported straight into paradise.

Sunflowers by Vincent van Gogh, c. 1888

And with your wife you will not be lonely any more, which I could wish for our sister as well. That, after your own marriage, is what I should set my heart on more than anything.

Please realise that I shall be very happy when your marriage has taken place. Look here now, if for your wife's sake it would perhaps be as well to have a picture of mine from time to time at Goupil's, then I will give up my grudge against them in this way.

I said I did not want to go back to them with too naïve a picture. But if you like you can exhibit the two pictures of sunflowers.

Gauguin would be glad to have one, and I should very much like to give Gauguin a real pleasure. So if he wants one of the two canvases, all right, I will do one of them over again, whichever he likes.

You will see that these canvases will catch the eye. But I would advise you to keep them for yourself, just for your own private pleasure and that of your wife. It is a kind of painting which rather changes in character, and takes on a richness the longer you look at it.

You know the peony is Jeannin's, the hollyhock belongs to Quost, but the sunflower is somewhat my own.

And after all I should like to go on exchanging my things with Gauguin even if sometimes it would cost me also rather dear.

The delay of the money was pure chance, and neither you nor I could do anything about it. A handshake.

Yours,
Vincent

from *The Letters of Vincent Van Gogh*
edited by Mark Roskill

Glossary

Goupil The Paris art dealers for whom Theo Van Gogh worked (Vincent had also worked for them)
Roulin A postman in Arles who befriended Van Gogh and who posed for portraits, as did his son Armand

Roulin's wife The subject of a series of paintings entitled *La Berceuse* (woman rocking a cradle), although all that can be seen of the cradle is the rope attached to it, in the woman's hand
'The Bedroom' *Van Gogh's Bedroom at Arles*

Read on!

1 From the letter, what can you deduce about Vincent Van Gogh, including his past, and about recent events in his life?
2 What does the letter tell you about Van Gogh's state of health and about his way of life at that time?
3 What does the letter reveal about Vincent Van Gogh's brother and about the relationship between the two brothers?
4 What do you think the following mean:

a) 'I am now safe until the arrival of your letter after the 1st'?
b) 'my sunflowers'?
c) 'everyone will now be afraid of me'?

Refer to books about Vincent Van Gogh.

5 List the main points made in the letter. How can you tell that these points are important?

Write on!

1 The language of the letter is conversational, but slightly more formal than speech.

a) Which words and phrases in particular might be used in a conversation?
b) How do the personal pronouns add to the conversational effect?
c) Which words and phrases sound more formal than speech?

2 The letter does more than communicate information, thanks and good wishes. What opinions, hopes and fears does it reveal?

Opinions	Hopes	Fears

3 Re-write the letter, communicating only information, with no explanations or expressions of feelings. Compare this with the original.

Re-write any sentences conveying information if they also contain explanations or expressions of feelings.

Over to you!

a) Make notes about what Theo might have written in his reply to the letter.
b) Write a reply from Theo, answering Vincent's questions and commenting on his news, opinions, hopes and fears.

Use a conversational style, but slightly more formal than speech.

22 Transcripts of conversations

This is the transcript of a recorded conversation between two friends who live in different parts of the country and so do not see one another often.

Karen: Hello.

Jane: Hi. It's Jane. Just wondered if you're snowed in. … Saw it on the news.

Karen: Hello, Jane. … No. It's not too bad. The worst bit's after the snow-plough goes past.

Jane: Snow-plough!?

Karen: Yes! One came past just before I got home. They do the two roads — you know the ones on each side of the village? They have to go through the village to get from one to the other. They make a huge wall across the driveways. I'll have to get a decent shovel.

Jane: Snowed out, instead of snowed in!

Karen: Ha … yes!

Jane: Dan and Sue were coming down for the weekend but they had to put it off. Their road's covered in ice. Oh … did I tell you they're grandparents?

Karen: No. When? A boy or a girl?

Jane: A girl. Laura … They're so thrilled … Hang on … John's just … Oh yes … something else I meant to tell you — Alan Smith died, or so Rod told John, and no one would make that up … I don't know when … quite a while. He'd moved to London, so no one knew. John bumped into Rod in Sainsbury's. You get all the news there. I think he'd been ill for a while.

Karen: No. What a shame. He wasn't very old.

Jane: No … only sixty.

Karen: I wonder if all this exercise does any good in the end?

Jane: It's OK as long as you don't overdo it. I'm still walking for half an hour every day.

Karen: That reminds me. Why don't we fix the date for you to come over? Some good walks. You need boots, though.

Jane: Oh, yes, that's why I phoned you back. Maybe … the four … no, we're going to Wales … er … oh … on the fourteenth … for the weekend … but the weekend after that … oh … no … we're going to stay with Dan and Sue. When's best for you?

Karen: I'll just check … mmmm. What about … I've dropped the diary … er … no … er … yes … the 28th? The weather might be better by then.

Jane: Mmmm. Yes, that's fine … Oh, just a … er, I'll need to check if Sue can come over … to stay with Mum.

Karen: How is your mum?

Jane: Just the same. She can't be left on her own. She's so worried that she's a burden. I keep telling her about all the things she actually helps us with … she's so patient with fiddly things like shelling peas … and polishing silver (well, silver plated tin!) … and she can still sew … and we like having her here.

Karen: Give her my best wishes.

Jane: Yes … just a … Mum … Oh … Yes … she sends hers.

Karen: So … let me know, when you've spoken to Sue. If not … maybe next month … I think … yes … there's one weekend.

Jane: Yes. She said she could … probably … any weekend this month. Look forward to it. I'll phone back later … or tomorrow … if I catch her. 'Bye.

Karen: 'Bye.

Read on!

1   What facts are revealed by the conversation?
2   What do you find out about Jane and Karen's opinions and feelings?
3   What can you guess is going on, apart from Jane and Karen talking to one another, during certain parts of the conversation?
4   How does Karen signal that she is going to end the conversation?
5   Using your answers from questions 1 and 2, write a brief summary of the conversation, using indirect speech where appropriate.

6   What are the main characteristics of the language of conversation which are different from written language? Think about: sentences, contractions, unnecessary ('filler') words and personal pronouns. Activity Sheet 22 will help.
7   Re-write the first twenty-one lines of the conversation, using complete sentences and without the 'filler' words. What effect does this have?

> Make the summary as brief as possible, using complete sentences.

Write on!

1   a) List the main pieces of information which Jane gave to Karen during the phone call.
    b) Write this information in the form of an email.
    c) Write Karen's reply in the form of an email.
2   If the text were to be used as part of a playscript, what would have to be added to it to help the people producing and performing it?

Giving an appearance of authenticity does not mean reproducing real life. This could be very boring for the audience.

> Think about the audience and purpose of the conversation and a playscript.

3   What kinds of changes, deletions and additions would a dramatist have to make to the words spoken by the characters?

Over to you!

1   Re-read the letter from Vincent Van Gogh to his brother Theo (**Unit 21**) and the reply you wrote from Theo.

Imagine how the brothers' conversation might have gone if they had been able to telephone one another.

a) Change the words of Van Gogh's letter to speech and mark where he might have stopped speaking to allow his brother to answer.
b) Write the replies which Theo might have made.
2   Write a 'transcript' of the brothers' conversation.

23 An explanation

The sense of smell: how it works

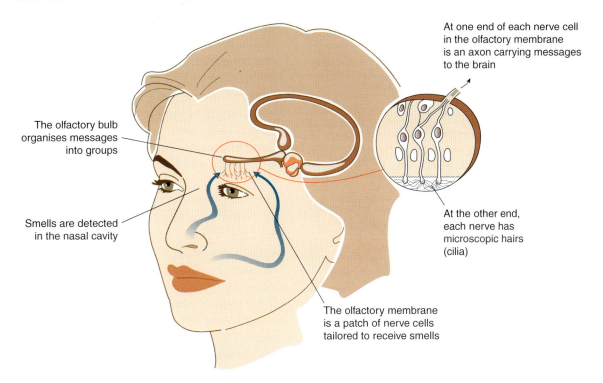

At one end of each nerve cell in the olfactory membrane is an axon carrying messages to the brain

The olfactory bulb organises messages into groups

Smells are detected in the nasal cavity

At the other end, each nerve has microscopic hairs (cilia)

The olfactory membrane is a patch of nerve cells tailored to receive smells

Sight and hearing are physical senses; they respond to the physical stimuli of light and sound waves. But smell and taste are chemical senses. Molecules actually have to enter our bodies through our noses for us to smell things.

Let's say you are walking through a pine forest, inhaling that pure, cool air. What happens is that some of the pine tree is volatile enough to vaporise and float free in the air. As you breathe in, those pine molecules are sucked into your nose and wafted to the nasal cavity at the back of the nostrils behind the bridge of the nose. When you chew something, odour molecules are pushed up another passage at the back of the mouth to the same nasal cavity so that food can be thoroughly smelled as well. Ninety per cent of the taste of foods is, in fact, from smell.

Here, in the nasal cavity, is the scent receptor site, composed of a special membrane of neurons (nerve cells) covered in a yellow-brown mucus. This membrane is called the olfactory epithelium. For us to smell something, it must reach this membrane; this is why we cannot smell when a cold blocks the membrane. In humans its total area is about 5 cm^2. Dogs have an olfactory epithelium twelve times bigger than ours; sharks have one of 2.2 m^2, while in rabbits the area roughly equals the skin surface of their entire bodies.

There are some smells we can detect at one part per trillion, like the green smell of vegetables – a primary food source. We can detect methyl mercaptan at 1/400 billionth of a gram per litre of air. This is the chemical, mixed with odourless natural gas, which helps us to detect a leak. It is also the characteristic odour of rotting flesh – probably the reason why we are so sensitive to it.

Waving through the mucous membrane like sea-grass at the bottom of the sea are millions of microscopic hairs called cilia.

An explanation

Every neuron in the olfactory epithelium sprouts several of these cilia, which are the nerve endings for gathering smells. These nerve endings are like the brain's furthest outposts into the world, the one place where, naked except for a little mucus, the brain itself sticks a periscope up into the outside world and samples it direct. Because these are the only neurons out in the open, they are also the only ones which can die and replace themselves; they do this every month or so.

The microscopic nerve-hairs (cilia) are packed with special receptor proteins. What happens next is still being elucidated. Basically, proteins on the receptor cilia bind only with the molecules of certain odours. It's like a highly complex jigsaw puzzle. Each receptor protein has a particular shape so that only matching pieces of the smell puzzle can fit into it. Smell X can waft over receptor proteins A, B, C and D, but only when it finds receptor X, with the right shape, will it lock into it and start the process which allows it to be smelled. When all the X-shaped sites are filled, we temporarily lose the ability to smell X, until enough of the X scent molecules are metabolised by the body. This is why we stop smelling a fragrance soon after we apply it.

When an odorant molecule meets the correct matching receptor protein on the cilia, the receptor protein itself reacts by changing shape, thus altering the property of the nerve cell. This prompts the cascade of chemical changes, then electrical changes, which are fired back towards the olfactory bulb in the brain to be registered as a particular smell. This bulb, about the size of a small berry, acts as a sorting house, organising the smell signals into groups on their way into other parts of the brain.

Whereas another theory once held that we have different receptors for lemon, orange and jasmine, it is now known that, say, orange, which is a complex of many odour chemicals, initiates not a single signal but a specific pattern of signals which may resemble tangerine, but are not exactly the same. The different odour chemicals in the orange bond with different protein receptors and it is the characteristic pattern of signals this produces which allows you to recognise orange compared with tangerine. It's a bit like Turkish carpets – they all have a similar pattern but each one is subtly different.

This pattern-method allows your nose to approach a completely new smell the way your immune system does a new microbe: by analysing it piecemeal. When attacking a pathogen, the immune system sends out many different antibody proteins, each of which can latch on to one small specific area of the enemy. In the same way, the nose examines a new smell from a multiplicity of different angles, each receptor clicking with ones of its particular chemical signatures, so that the olfactory bulb gradually builds up a picture of its characteristic pattern to be recognised in future as 'smell of new car' or 'smell of plastic toy'.

from *Perfume: The Creation and Allure of Classic Fragrances* by Susan Irvine

Read on!

1   What is the main difference between physical and chemical senses?

2   List the scientific and technical words which the passage introduces and whose meanings it explains.

3   a)   For which of the following words do you know the meaning? For which can you work out the meaning from their context, and which do you need to look up?

antibody, epithelium, immune system, membrane, molecule, mucus, olfactory, pathogen, protein, receptor, stimuli, vaporise, volatile

Scientific and technical words in the passage		
Meanings are known	Meanings can be worked out from context	Words need to be looked up

b)   Explain the meanings of the words.

4   List the four analogies used to explain complex processes:

Analogy	Process
1	
2	

5   The passage helps you to understand new ideas by linking them to your existing knowledge and understanding. Describe three examples of this.

6   Describe another way in which the passage helps you to understand the complexity of the sense of smell.

Write on!

1   Re-read the passage and make notes about each stage in the process of smelling a perfume.

- Use a flow chart.
- Give each stage a heading.

2   Write a summary of the passage, saying what the reader can find out from it and how helpful it is.

Limit your summary to 50 words.

Over to you!

1   Read through some of your own work in which you have explained a complex process. The audience was probably your teacher (who already understands it). Imagine someone else reading it.

a)   Make a note of any words whose meanings need to be made clear.

b)   Note any analogies you could use to help the reader to understand the process.

2   Re-write your explanation for someone to whom the process is new. Model your writing on the style of the passage, using diagrams and analogies to help the reader make links between new and existing ideas.

24   A discussion

This article appeared in The Week *during the week following the first Holocaust Memorial Day.*

Holocaust Day: a piece of Labour hypocrisy?

'Civilisation lives by memory,' said Britain's Chief Rabbi Jonathan Sacks in *The Times*. 'What we forget, we can repeat. What we remember, we can guard against.' That's why Britain's first Holocaust Memorial Day, which took place last week, was such a good idea. Held on the 56th anniversary of the liberation of Auschwitz, the day commemorated the victims of Nazi genocide as well as persecuted minorities everywhere. Events were held around the country; in London, Tony Blair stood alongside Prince Charles in the Palace of Westminster to listen to speeches from celebrities including Ian McKellen and Bob Geldof.

Of course we must remember the victims of the holocaust, said Anne Karpf in the *Sunday Express*. But, as the daughter of a concentration camp survivor, I have 'profound reservations' about the idea of a special day. What can it possibly have achieved? The Government hoped the memorial would promote racial tolerance. But while there are lessons to be drawn from history, finding 'lessons for living' from circumstances as extreme as genocide is a completely different matter. 'Searching for the common denominator in such different historical events leaves you nothing but a set of absurd liberal truisms, such as 'be nice to each other' and 'don't bully'.' For all the academic research, the Holocaust remains 'essentially unfathomable'. It's hard to imagine that the children 'forced to feign sadness' on this commemorative day had more than 'a glancing understanding of why'.

The problem, said Nick Cohen in the *New Statesman*, is one of overexposure.

Images of the Holocaust have become so ubiquitous that they have lost any real meaning. The genocide itself has been appropriated by everyone from feminists to artists as a 'two-dimensional icon' of suffering. New Labour justified the memorial on the grounds that remembrance would make us more 'sensitive' to oppression in the future. In fact, the opposite is true. 'The Holocaust was such an extreme event that modern injustices can be dismissed as paltry in comparison.' New Labour is especially guilty of this, said *The Guardian*. Consider this piece of hypocrisy: the memorial day was sponsored by the Government, and both the Prime Minister and Home Secretary gave heartfelt speeches about the need to 'oppose racism and anti-Semitism, victimisation and genocide'. But these admirable sentiments are quite at odds with New Labour's Draconian asylum policy. The Jewish victims of Hitler's persecution would not have been welcomed into Blair's Britain.

from *The Week*,
3 February 2001

The Labyrinth of Names at the Holocaust Memorial, Yad Vashem, Jerusalem

Read on!

1. What views are presented to support or oppose the introduction of a Holocaust Memorial Day in Britain?

Views supporting the Memorial Day	Views opposing the Memorial Day

2. Which opponents of the Memorial Day agree with some of the reasons *for* it? With which reasons do they agree?
3. For what kind of audience is this article written? How can you tell?
4. The article includes many compound and complex sentences.

Think about age, level of education, reading level and interests.

a) Give examples of complex sentences used in the article:

Examples of compound sentences	Examples of complex sentences

b) Re-write the article using simple sentences.
c) Compare this with the original version.

- *A simple sentence has one clause.*
- *A compound sentence has two or more main clauses (each of which could be used as an independent sentence).*
- *A complex sentence has at least one main clause with one or more subordinate clauses.*

Write on!

1. How is the use of quotations in this article similar to, and different from, reported speech?

Consider how much of what the people said or wrote is included and how it is combined with the surrounding text.

2. a) Re-write the passage, converting all the reported speech into indirect speech. You could first scan the text into a word-processor, for speed.
   b) What was the effect of these changes, especially on the opening sentence?
   c) Which version do you think was the more effective, and why?
3. What makes the headline particularly suitable for the article?

Over to you!

1. Look for an issue which has been widely reported in newspapers recently.
   a) Make notes about what the different journalists (and the people they interview) say about the issue.
   b) Organise your notes on a chart (as in **Read on!** Question 1) under headings which indicate the different opinions expressed in the newspapers.
   c) Write a sentence or two to summarise the opinion you have formed of the issue.
2. Write a discussion which would fit into the same column space as the article about Holocaust Memorial Day (400 words).

- *Use quotations in the same way.*
- *Think of an opening sentence which will make the reader want to read on.*
- *Think of a headline which will both attract the reader's attention and indicate your opinion.*

25 Advice

This is from a leaflet produced by the Department of Health. You can read the entire leaflet on the Department of Health website: www.doh.gov.uk/kwkw.

Keep warm, dress well

There's an increased risk of becoming ill if you get cold, outdoors as well as at home. These simple steps will help to protect you.

At home

Wear several thin layers of clothes rather than one thick layer – the warmth from your body will get trapped between the layers.

Choose clothes made with wool, cotton, or fleecy synthetic fibres that are designed to be light and warm.

In the coldest weather, a good way to keep warm in bed is to wear bed socks and a night cap or scarf round your head, as well as thermal underwear and a warm nightdress or pyjamas.

Outdoors

Several thinner layers of clothing under your coat will keep you warmer than one thick layer.

Wear something on your head, otherwise you'll get cold very quickly.

Wear warm, dry, flat, non-slip shoes or boots, especially in frosty weather.

Winter warmth advice line →

Keep warm, eat well

Food is fuel, it helps keep you warm. Follow these suggestions for eating well this winter.

Aim to have at least one hot meal a day and have hot drinks regularly through the day.

Have a hot drink before bedtime.

Prepare a thermos flask of a hot drink to have by your bed in case you wake up in the night feeling cold.

Include something from each of the five main food groups in what you eat each day:

Group 1: bread, cereals, potatoes, pasta, chapatis

Group 2: fresh fruit and vegetables (try to have at least five portions during the course of each day)

Group 3: milk and dairy foods

Group 4: meat, fish, eggs, peas and pulses such as beans (including baked beans)

Group 5: foods containing fat and sugar

Try to keep a stock of food from all these groups in case you can't get out to the shops in very cold weather. **If you are on a special diet, talk to your doctor before you make any change in what you eat or drink.**

8am to 8pm Monday to Friday

from the Department of Health website:
www.doh.gov.uk/kwkw

Read on!

1 a) How formal is the language in this leaflet, on a scale of 1 to 4?

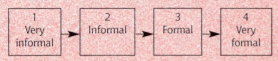

| 1 Very informal | 2 Informal | 3 Formal | 4 Very formal |

Consider: vocabulary, personal pronouns, contractions, verb form and mood.

b) Explain your answer to (a).
c) Why is this type of language used?

2 How complex is the language?

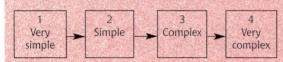

| 1 Very simple | 2 Simple | 3 Complex | 4 Very complex |

Consider: vocabulary and the number of phrases and clauses in each sentence.

3 What can you deduce about the intended audience for this leaflet, and how?

Consider: subject matter, layout, font style, font size.

4 To which parts of the text is your attention drawn, and why? How is this achieved?

5 Make notes about the layout of the leaflet: paragraphing, headings, sub-headings and other organisational devices, indentations, use of colour, font sizes and styles.

Write on!

1 The leaflet addresses the reader as 'you', but it is clearly addressed to a large group of people unknown to the writer.

a) Re-write the two pages in impersonal language which refers to readers as 'people', 'they' and 'he or she'.
b) What difference does this change make to the tone of the leaflet?

Explain why personal language was used.

2 What makes the advice in this leaflet sound authoritative and convincing, despite the use of informal language?

Re-read the passage and notice how each piece of advice is backed up.

Over to you!

a) Read, and make notes from books, magazines, newspapers and websites on maintaining a healthy weight.
b) Organise the information according to topic (or questions). Use the Activity Sheet.
c) Using a word-processor or desktop publishing program, design a leaflet which presents the information in a way which will appeal to people of your own age.

Think about:

- number and size of pages
- layout features: font, illustrations, graphs and charts, headings, sub-headings, bullet points, arrows, boxes, and so on.
- language: how formal, personal and complex.

26 Controversy

The history of life on earth has been a history of interaction between living things and their surroundings. To a large extent, the physical form and the habits of the earth's vegetation and its animal life have been moulded by the environment. Considering the whole span of earthly time, the opposite effect, in which life actually modifies its surroundings, has been relatively slight. Only within the moment of time represented by the present century has one species – man – acquired significant power to alter the nature of his world.

During the past quarter-century this power has not only increased to one of disturbing magnitude but it has changed in character. The most alarming of all man's assaults upon the environment is the contamination of air, earth, rivers, and sea with dangerous and even lethal materials. This pollution is for the most part irrecoverable; the chain of evil it initiates not only in the world that must support life but in living tissues is for the most part irreversible. In this now universal contamination of the environment, chemicals are the sinister and little-recognised partners of radiation in changing the very nature of the world – the very nature of its life. Strontium, released through nuclear explosions into the air, comes to earth in rain or drifts down as fallout, lodges in soil, enters into the grass or corn or wheat grown there, and in time takes up its abode in the bones of a human being, there to remain until his death. Similarly, chemicals sprayed on

Controversy

croplands or forests or gardens lie long in soil, entering into living organisms, passing from one to another in a chain of poisoning and death. Or they pass mysteriously by underground streams until they emerge and, through the alchemy of air and sunlight, combine into new forms that kill vegetation, sicken cattle, and work unknown harm on those who drink from once-pure wells. As Albert Schweitzer has said, 'Man can hardly even recognise the devils of his own creation.'

It took hundreds of millions of years to produce the life that now inhabits the earth – aeons of time in which that developing and evolving and diversifying life reached a state of adjustment and balance with its surroundings. The environment, rigorously shaping and directing the life it supported, contained elements that were hostile as well as supporting. Certain rocks gave out dangerous radiation; even within the light of the sun, from which all life draws its energy, there were short-wave radiations with power to injure. Given time – time not in years but in millennia – life adjusts, and a balance has been reached. For time is the essential ingredient; but in the modern world there is no time.

The rapidity of change and the speed with which new situations are created follows the impetuous and heedless pace of man rather than the deliberate pace of nature. Radiation is no longer merely the background radiation of rocks, the bombardment of cosmic rays, the ultra-violet of the sun that have existed before there was any life on earth; radiation is now the unnatural creation of man's tampering with the atom. The chemicals to which life is asked to make its adjustment are no longer merely the calcium and silica and copper and all the rest of the minerals washed out of the rocks and carried in rivers to the sea; they are the synthetic creations of man's inventive mind, brewed in his laboratories, and having no counterparts in nature.

To adjust to these chemicals would require time on the scale that is nature's; it would require not merely the years of a man's life but the life of generations. And even this, were it by some miracle possible, would be futile, for new chemicals come from our laboratories in an endless stream.

from *Silent Spring* by Rachel Carson

Read on!

1 Why is pollution such an important issue for people today? Give some examples which affect you directly.
2 Which aspects of environmentalism do you support and which do you not? Give your reasons.
3 Why is the earth so polluted today, according to this passage?

4 Whom, or what does Rachel Carson blame for pollution?
5 How might an industrialist respond to Rachel Carson's argument?
6 How does time affect rates of pollution? Make notes from the passage.

In the past	At the present time

Write on!

1 Draw a diagram to show what Rachel Carson means by 'the chain of evil'.

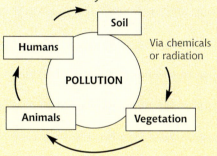

The Activity Sheet provides an alternative.

2 Explain what happened in the natural world before people produced so many pollutants. Why can it not cope with the new ones?
3 Write two additional paragraphs to continue this passage, concentrating on a particular environment which is in danger of pollution: for example, the sea, the atmosphere, rainforests, Antarctica. You may need to research to find examples.

Over to you!

1 What can be done to halt the damage being done to the earth and to our immediate environment? Make notes before you write.

What is damaging the environment	What can be done to stop this

Write your response as either:

• a leaflet, or
• a magazine article.

Whichever format you choose, decide upon your audience and their requirements.

2 Collect images from magazines and leaflets from environmental agencies (for instance, Greenpeace) or from the Internet which examine the most extreme examples of pollution in the world. Create a gallery of these, either on the school web site or in the class, and label them with key statements to spark controversy.

• Use email to write a series of responses between classmates or pupils from other schools.

27 Commenting

The problem pill

Many people have a principled, usually religious, objection to abortion. Of these, most extend their opposition to the morning-after Pill, which, if conception has taken place, works by effectively killing the embryo. Such people will have clear-cut views about the decision to allow chemists to stock what is, in their eyes, an abortifacient.

A rather larger group of people, while not objecting to the morning-after Pill *per se*, will none the less feel uneasy about its increasing availability. Setting aside, for a moment, any moral qualms, there are good reasons to worry about the health effects. Though the jury is still out, medical evidence has cleared, on the whole, the contraceptive Pill. But no one has comprehensively tested the impact of frequent doses of the morning-after Pill, which packs a much heavier hormonal punch. When the morning-after Pill was available only on prescription, women were unlikely to use it regularly. But it will now be easy, by visiting several pharmacists, to amass a large supply. There is bound to be a temptation for some teenage girls to treat the morning-after Pill as a form of regular contraception.

By the same token, a girl who finds herself, say, two months pregnant may conclude that a large dose of the morning-after Pill is the easiest way to induce an abortion. Again, disregarding any religious objections, this is also worrying on health grounds. These are not arguments of principle, but they are no less important for that. The need to visit a doctor imbued the taking of the morning-after Pill with a gravity which was both medical and moral. Popping into Boots for a pill which will make your womb unable to hold a foetus can only have the effect of devaluing the life-giving process. Just as a rising number of abortions in Britain seems to have coincided with a decline in respect for life in general, so the ease with which the morning-after Pill can be purchased will surely lead to a further trivialisation of sexual relations.

Thirty years ago, when Parliament passed the Abortion Act, David Steel and his supporters argued that the change would do away with back-street terminations. Who could have imagined that, by today, abortions would instead be purchased across the counter? It may be many years before we can assess the social consequences of this latest relaxation of the rules, but the prognosis is not good.

from *The Daily Telegraph*,
2 January 2001

Read on!

1 In the passage, what are the two main arguments against selling the morning-after Pill without prescription?
2 Which other argument is mentioned but is not discussed?
3 What points are raised to support each of the two main arguments?

Argument 1:	Argument 2:
Point 1	Point 1
Point 2	Point 2

4 What facts are needed to support the points you have listed?
5 What assumptions are made by the writer of the article:

a) about the women who are likely to use the morning-after Pill
b) about teenage girls?

6 The purpose of this article is to make a comment (which might lead to action) on an issue. What actions do you think the writer of the comment hopes for?
7 Consider the writer's language: what images do the following create?

killing, abortion, abortifacient, heavier hormonal punch, induce an abortion, a pill which will make your womb unable to hold a foetus, devaluing the life-giving process

Write on!

1 Find out, and make notes, about how the morning-after Pill works.
2 List any points which have been ignored by the writer of the passage
3 Write your own comment on the sale of the morning-after Pill.

Write about 250 words.

Write an introductory sentence or paragraph which tells the reader your view.

Think about a sentence to summarise what you have written.

Over to you!

1 Think about a new law or regulation which has been in the news recently.

a) Note your responses to it:

- the good which might come from it
- any concerns you have about it.

b) Decide whether you support or oppose it. List your reasons.

c) Focus on two or three main arguments. Under each argument list the points which support it; you could organise these on a chart (see **Read on!** Question 3).

2 Write a comment (about 250 words) about the introduction of the law or regulation. The Activity Sheet will help you to organise your ideas.

Think about the effect on the reader of the language you use.

28 Reviews

The Claim ***
Director: Michael Winterbottom
Starring: Peter Mullan, Milla Jovovich, Wes
   Bentley, Nastassja Kinski, Sarah Polley
Certificate: 15
Released: Friday 9 February 2001

By Damien Love

It is nearer the mark to describe Michael Winterbottom's tale as being *inspired by* Thomas Hardy's *The Mayor of Casterbridge*, rather than as an *adaptation* of the novel. Hardy provides the impetus – a drunk sells his wife and baby to another man, sobers up and prospers until, 18 years later, when he is a respected town boss, his wife and her child reappear, dragging the judgment he has been postponing passing on himself and an illusory chance at redemption. But Winterbottom ditches the plot, and transposes the action to the winter-bound foothills of the Sierra Nevada, years after the Californian goldrush of 1849.

Peter Mullan plays the fated protagonist, who traded his family for a mine which made him wealthy enough to build the desolate town of Kingdom Come. Milla Jovovich is the woman with whom Mullan has since taken up, a Portuguese brothel-owner, keening yearning, throaty ballads which mesmerise the bar-room each night. The trans-continental railroad is being built, and, coinciding with the reappearance of Mullan's wife and daughter, a group of surveyors, led by Wes Bentley, arrives in Kingdom Come, to ascertain whether the railway will pass through – a decision upon which the town s future depends.

Landscape is vital to Winterbottom's film, and one of the most important terrains is Mullan's face. A rare sight at the centre of a movie, Mullan looks like a man who has worked, marked by lines suggestive of heavy exertion, and the fear, anger and pride which can accompany it. He moves with the rigid grace of a body shaped by toil, and is good, too, at hinting mania in his eyes: it's the logic of years spent keeping what you have earned, in a place where there are no laws except those you are able to enforce yourself, along with flashes of guilt. Prisoner's eyes.

His wife (played by Nastassja Kinski) reappears, hacking up blood in wracking fits and asking that he agree to provide for their daughter when she dies. Kinski wanders in like a ghost, which is about right.

As her daughter, however, Sarah Polley is insubstantial in ways which are all wrong, characterising a strange remoteness which runs like a flaw through the film. It's as though the emotions of all involved had been numbed by the harsh weather. As the film passes, it gets hard to care much about what happens to any of these distant characters. Winterbottom is good with the physical reality of the place, though, and the location confers a great, stark beauty on his movie.

Filming under these heavy skies amid all this endless, blinding snow, with the dark wool of the clothes, the stained, battered wood of the town, and the trees like sharp pencil marks against the frozen hills, is as close to making a black-and-white film in colour as you can get.

Although *The Claim* is glorious to look at and aims toward the larger forces – destiny, fate, consequence – swirling around its characters, some human kind of warmth could have made it a much more memorable experience.

adapted from *The Scotsman*,
8 February 2001

Read on!

1 What does the reviewer say are the similarities and differences between the film *The Claim* and the novel which inspired it (*The Mayor of Casterbridge*)?

2 What do the following phrases mean?

'the judgement he has been postponing passing on himself', 'an illusory chance at redemption', 'keening yearning, throaty ballads', 'lines suggestive of heavy exertion', 'the rigid grace of a body shaped by toil', 'hacking up blood in wracking fits'

3 What does the reviewer say are the strengths and weaknesses of the film?

4 The review summarises the plot but does not give away too much.

a) What questions does this summary raise in the reader's mind?

b) From the summary of the storyline and the description of the characters and setting, what kind of ending do you expect the film to have, and why?

5 a) What initial impression do you have of the main character?

b) What is your impression of this character by the end of the review?

Write on!

1 Edit the first two paragraphs so that they describe only the storyline.

Describe the effect of this change.

Think about the impression the review makes on the reader about the atmosphere of the film.

2 Re-read the last two sentences of paragraph 5.

a) List the powerful words and phrases.

b) Describe how you would feel if you stepped into this setting.

3 Think of another film setting which you have found striking in some way.

a) In two or three words, what was the overall impression of the setting: for example, gentle and romantic; hot and sultry, exotic and exciting?

b) Note any powerful adjectives, nouns/noun phrases and verbs you could use to communicate the effect of the setting.

c) Write a paragraph to describe the setting of the film.

Over to you!

1 Make notes about a film you have seen which is based on a book.

a) Is it a straightforward film version of the book, an adaptation (perhaps in a different setting or time, or even a parody), or just inspired by the storyline of a book?

b) Did you like the film? Why? Organise your comments under headings: setting, casting, script, atmosphere, tempo. The Activity Sheet will help.

c) List its strengths and weaknesses.

2 a) Write an outline of the storyline.

b) Decide how much of the storyline you should reveal to the reader.

c) Note any details to include to raise questions in the reader's mind. (See **Read on!** Question 5.)

3 Write a 450-word review of the film. The Activity Sheet will help.

29 Arguing a point of view

These are edited emails from the website of the Today *programme on BBC Radio 4. The programme broadcast extracts from a recording made by one of its reporters, Mike Thomson, during a night spent tracking a cat in Bristol to find out about the mammals and birds it killed.*

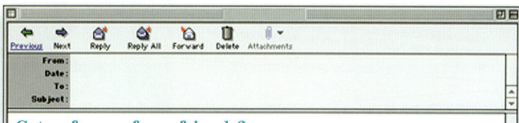

Previous Next Reply Reply All Forward Delete Attachments

From:
Date:
To:
Subject:

Cats – foes or furry friends?

Chris Mead from the British Trust for Ornithology, one of the contributors to a *Today* debate heard this week on whether or not a 'cat cull' is needed, writes:

I am a cat lover but the carnage in our countryside of small birds and mammals – at almost 300,000 deaths a year – is an insult to our conservation credentials. If we had real wild cats in the countryside in Britain there would only be a few tens of thousands rather than the 9,000,000 pet cats we now have. Neutering all but those cats from which we want to breed is the first step we should take.

   The main problem is not pet cats but the hordes of feral cats which roam the towns and countryside making a living on whatever they can catch. It is not their fault that they catch a rare bird, a dormouse or a bat, but they should not be there to do it. I would advocate their eradication, mostly through trapping and humane destruction – collars, tattoos or microchips would identify those with loving owners. However, out in the depths of the countryside it might mean that some had to be shot – for the good of the real wildlife. The decline of birds is not being driven by cat predation – habitat loss is much more important – but losses to cats are not acceptable.

Vanessa Bransden 09:06am Mon 12 Feb 01
My solution to the problem of cats killing birds and mammals is to keep them in at night. I have two cats and they come in at night. In the morning we let them out, so at night they kill nothing. Occasionally we have the odd mouse or vole killed in the daytime, but not as many as if the cats were out hunting all night. It is a shame that people are still not prepared to recognise their own part in the decline of wildlife and instead blame a companion animal which does so much to enhance people's lives. A study by the British Trust for Ornithology a couple of years ago showed that at least 10 million deaths of birds in Britain are caused by traffic. Moreover, changes in farming methods with the increased use of pesticides and the destruction of hedgerows can be seen to be far more harmful. A report by the Game Conservancy Trust and Sussex University showed that corn buntings have declined by 74% in the last 25 years because of intensive farming leading to the loss of food and habitats.
My fear is that the hysterical bias will only encourage people to think it is acceptable to persecute and harm this popular pet.

Elizabeth Astley 09:31pm Mon 12 Feb 01
Cats should be neutered wherever possible and they should be kept in at night for the cat's safety, but has the world gone completely mad? Are we now discouraging cats from following their natural instincts? It is irresponsible to talk of culling cats; before long we shall have every cat-hater taking pot-shots at them.

Sybil Chick 08:21pm Tue 13 Feb 01
This morning we heard that the rat population was increasing, bringing with it diseases. Surely then we should be encouraging our cats to do something about it!

Arguing a point of view

Keith Elliott 11:21am Mon 05 Feb 01
Cats kill for pleasure, not for food. They toy with their prey for their own satisfaction. Get rid of them before we lose essential small animals from our countryside. Cull, please!

Robin Bailey 09:56am Mon 12 Feb 01
How do people think cats survived before the invention of overpriced pet food and electrically-heated beds? Much better to have cats as pets, neutered and well-fed, than in uncontrolled feral packs.

Virginia C 08:38am Thu 08 Feb 01
We all know that statistics are easily manufactured, so why this outburst of anti- and pro-cat on the basis of a few quoted figures? Why cull any creature?

Debbie Hogben 07:07pm Tue 06 Feb 01
Keith Elliot's message is full of anthropomorphism – cats do not have a concept of killing for 'fun': this is a word we understand in relation to human behaviour. It takes a long evolutionary period for instinctive (conditioned) behaviour to be eliminated. The domestication of cats in the evolutionary scale is relatively recent. There was a time when killing prey was vital for survival and it will be many, many thousands of years before it will evolve out of cats which do not need to kill for food.

Philippa Manasseh 12:14pm Mon 05 Feb 01
In 1665 with plague raging, the destruction of all cats and dogs in London was authorised, as was then common practice. That was good news for the rats and mice. The plague continued, spread by fleas on rats. Rats and mice cause more health problems than cats. Cats give enormous pleasure to some people, but do they really do any serious harm?

Barry Blatt 12:19am Tue 06 Feb 01
There is a balance struck between predator and prey, which we have seriously disturbed by feeding cats food out of tins and keeping them in warm houses. In the wild, cats would catch some small mammals, as would, say, owls and hawks, but their population would be limited by their hunting ability. By creating an over-population of cats we are making it tough on the mice, and for the other predators which rely on mice for food.
The serious decline in wild mammals is partly due to environmental problems, but we have in recent years done a fair bit about this. If the mammals are still decreasing, then I'm afraid there is a major suspect purring on your carpet. Time to cut down its numbers.

Robin Roper 01:05pm Mon 05 Feb 01
'Vermin' defines a species which threatens or causes damage to human health and/or economic activity. A broader definition includes a species which, because of population imbalance, deleteriously affects other populations and the overall ecosystem. If the brown rat, magpie, grey squirrel, feral mink and red fox are vermin, then why should cats, in such great numbers, be considered as anything but vermin in need of responsible control?
I prefer to see animals wild and free in healthy natural ecosystems; I do not begrudge the sparrow hawk its meal of a blue tit or the barn owl its meal of a field vole. Domestic cats are alien predators present in unnatural numbers, and doing a lot of predation. Cats are also fed by their owners; their predation is a hobby, not a means of survival. The barn owl does not have such luxury and every field vole caught by a cat could be the loss of a meal for a barn owl. If people must have cats, then please – one only, kept under control and neutered.

Read on!

1. Organise the views presented in the emails under three main headings:

Cull cats	Neuter	Neither cull nor neuter

2. Whose arguments are supported by evidence, and what evidence do they quote?

Argument	Evidence

3. List any words and phrases in the arguments which you recognise as 'the language of argument', for example 'so', 'therefore', 'naturally', 'on the other hand'.

4. List any words or phrases which suggest that:

   a) the present situation is unnatural
   b) cats are pests.

5. List any words or phrases which express the idea that:

   a) the presence of cats is beneficial
   b) cats are harmless.

Write on!

1. List any useful 'argument' words you think of which did not appear in the text. (See **Read on!** question 3.)

2. In the arguments against the culling or compulsory neutering of cats, what alternatives are offered for protecting small birds and mammals from cats?

   Evaluate those arguments according to the responses in the emails. (Which were supported by evidence of some kind? Which consisted of opinion only?)

3. a) Write one sentence to summarise the collective opinions of the people who wrote the emails.

   b) Write an argument which supports or opposes the culling or compulsory neutering of cats. Use your answers from **Read On!**

Over to you!

1. Read the emailed responses on a current topic on either 'Talking point' or 'Argue' on BBC Radio 4's *Today* website: www.bbc.co.uk/radio4/. Also read the item which began the debate.

   a) Copy some of the emails about the issue and paste them on to a Word document.

   b) Give the text a heading and a sub-heading which sets it in its context.

2. Organise the emails on a chart under the headings 'for' or 'against'.

3. Note your own ideas about the issue, do some research to support your point of view, and place these ideas and data on the chart.

4. Plan your argument, using Activity Sheet 28.

5. Edit and refine your argument, clarifying it and adding emphasis where it is needed. Present the finished argument.

You can achieve clarity and emphasis by repetition and with devices such as italics, bold, capital letters, sub-headings and bullet points.

30 Promotion

This text is adapted from a speech by Ann Widdecombe, the Shadow Home Secretary, during a Conservative Party conference.

Ann Widdecombe

My team and I have been listening carefully to the debate today. It reflects the debate [on law and order] that is going on across this country. It has shown the overriding need for Common Sense in the way we approach issues such as law and order.

We need to build a more secure society.

I make a direct link between the rising crime rate and Labour's disgraceful treatment of the police service in this country. Labour's manifesto said 'The police have our strong support. We will get more officers back on the beat.' Their promises on the police – like so many of their promises – have been empty ones. They have said one thing and done another. The statistics tell a sorry tale. Police funding cut last year, standing still this year and a tiny increase of just 0.3 per cent next year.

We will have to wait until after the next election before Labour's cuts to police funding are reversed. There are also fewer police officers – more than 1,000 fewer. Recruitment down by a fifth. Some forces have not been recruiting at all because of lack of money. The thin blue line is getting thinner. Last week, Jack Straw announced 16,000 police recruits over the next three years. What he didn't say was that over the last three years, total recruitment has been 18,000!

Labour have said one thing and done another. Jack Straw and Tony Blair promised to be tough on crime – but instead they have been tough on the crime-fighters. That's not Common Sense.

We will provide whatever money it takes to reverse the cuts in police numbers that have happened – and will happen – under Labour. This reflects the importance the people of this country, and we in the Conservative Party, place on law and order. Unlike Labour, who have cut police funding and presided over rising crime rates. Labour's gaps in the thin blue line must be filled – and after the next election we will do just that.

We will also undertake a comprehensive review of the way in which this country is policed. The police can't do everything at once, and you simply cannot have a police officer on every street corner – yet we all have massive expectations of the police. Too many police officers are still spending too much time on things other than fighting crime. Not just form-filling, but other duties, such as escorting wide loads, for which highly trained, highly skilled crime-fighters are not essential. Coupled with our pledge to reverse Labour's cuts, we will get more officers back on the beat.

We will look at the problems of policing rural areas. Many police stations are miles from the communities they serve, leading to high response times that, in turn, make crime, and the fear of crime, into a serious problem. We need faster response times and more visible policing, returning the feeling of local law enforcement to our countryside. Why should rural people have to wait more than twice as long as those in urban areas before they receive a police response to an emergency call? Putting more officers into rural communities will ensure that our countryside is safer. That's plain Common Sense.

Jack Straw's response to rising prison numbers is to let prisoners out early. Under Labour, criminals sentenced to six months are getting out on an electronic tag in just six weeks. Worse still, these criminals re-offend while they are on the tag. Persistent criminals need tough sentences – which is why we are proposing mandatory sentences for those peddling drugs to children. We must give prisons a purpose. Private prisons have been leading the way. A recent Home Office study concluded that they provide more purposeful activity. Work in prison makes sure that the system is not a 'soft touch'. It also helps the rehabilitation of prisoners by providing them with the skills to help them lead purposeful crime-free lives outside. Rehabilitation is not a soft option – it is a way to protect the public.

Too many prisoners spend too much time doing too little. Prison work will be real work – based on outside contracts and competing on an unsubsidised, commercial basis. The Treasury rules which currently make it impossible to reinvest profits from workshops will be relaxed. Prisoners will be paid a realistic wage – from which deductions will be made to cover some of the costs of their upkeep, money for their families on the outside, money for savings to help them adjust when they leave prison and money to help their victims recover from the effects of crime. We will institute a full working day in all prisons.

Labour said that their policy on youth crime was 'zero tolerance'. Anti-Social Behaviour Orders were to be their flagship – but just three have been issued against under 18s. No local child curfew orders have been issued. Perhaps that's where the 'zero' came from. They have even been forced to cancel the monitoring exercise for child curfews because there are no curfews to monitor! All this despite Labour's Crime and Disorder Act being on the statute book for over a year. Zero tolerance? Zero results. Zero Common Sense.

Too many young menaces are still out on our streets. Too many young offenders re-offend. A handful of young offenders commit over a quarter of all youth crime. Our policies to tackle youth crime address the real issues. We will increase the number of places in secure training centres tenfold. We will introduce new flexible detention orders ranging from six months to two years. But it's not just locking them up that's the solution. We need to provide them with a stable, constructive environment that encourages their rehabilitation. That's why we will also introduce one-stop justice for these younger offenders. They will no longer have to spend days travelling to court. They will be able to concentrate on their rehabilitation without the constant distraction of court appearances. Realistic targets will be set for each younger offender – such as an educational standard or even the basics, like simple good behaviour. And they will be given a real incentive to achieve those targets. If by the end of the minimum six month period they have achieved the target, they will be released. If not, they will have to serve the remainder of their sentence – up to two years.

Our measures will be effective and will tackle the causes of youth crime. They will punish younger offenders by depriving them of their liberty. They will deter them by providing a custodial sentence – not a soft option. They will rehabilitate them by taking them out of the environment that has failed them and giving them a real incentive to change. And they will protect the public by getting them off our streets. For too long, victims have been 'just another statistic'. That's Common Sense.

In the Conservative Party, the British people have a party which is listening to their concerns, which is backing the crime-fighters, which will address the real issues and which has a clear vision for the future. Tony Blair calls this 'Addams Family Values'. I call it Common Sense.

All of us, from the Shadow Cabinet to the newest member of the party, must go now and set out that vision.

Read on!

1   To what audience is this speech addressed? (Consider not just the audience where the speech was delivered, but others who hear or read it).

2   a)   What is the purpose of the speech?
    b)   How does the speaker attempt to convince the audience?

Attacking the Labour Party:	Promoting the Conservative Party:

   c)   Compare the speaker's methods of persuasion with those of advertisements. Which could not be used in advertisements? Why not?

3   How is a prepared speech different from the spoken words in a playscript?

How is it different from a telephone conversation?

Think about responses and replies.

4   Look at the length of the sentences in the speech. List the very short sentences and say how they tend to be used.

5   Consider the most effective way in which to deliver the speech.

   With a partner, practise reading it aloud, noting pauses and emphasis.

Do not try to mimic Ann Widdecombe's delivery, but think about what is being said and the most effective way in which to say it.

Write on!

1   The speaker does not list *every* Labour Party 'failure' concerning law and order, but she balances each one by stating how the Conservative Party will succeed. Show how the 'failures' are countered:

'Failure' by Labour	How the Conservatives will succeed
A cut in police funding	An increase in police funding

2   How does the speaker's language emphasise these comparisons?

   Consider words which 'echo' one another.

3   What does 'Addams family values' mean? Of what phrase (used by the Conservative Party) is it a parody? List other parodied phrases.

5   List examples of alliteration and metaphor which affect the delivery of the speech.

Over to you!

1   Think of something you would change if you were to become Prime Minister.

2   Say what is wrong with the present situation. Check your facts.

3   Describe the purpose of the changes (for instance, to improve public transport in rural areas) and list the actions to take (for instance, subsidise buses).

4   Plan a speech about the issue. The Activity Sheet will help.

5   Read your speech and underline anything to emphasise. Show how you will do this. For example, you could alter the length of a sentence or repeat a phrase at intervals throughout the speech.

Bear in mind the audience and how you hope they will respond to the speech.
Think about the impression you want to create.
*Your answers to **Write on!** will help.*